The Mini Mentor

The Power of Possibility:
Short Stories to Inspire and
Motivate Young Dreamers

Ava A.S. Jacobs
& Robert N. Jacobs

Grosvenor House
Publishing Limited

All rights reserved
Copyright © Ava A.S. Jacobs & Robert N. Jacobs, 2024

The right of Ava A.S. Jacobs & Robert N. Jacobs to be identified as the authors of this work has been asserted in accordance with Section 78 of the Copyright, Designs and Patents Act 1988

The book cover is copyright to
Ava A.S. Jacobs & Robert N. Jacobs

This book is published by
Grosvenor House Publishing Ltd
Link House
140 The Broadway, Tolworth, Surrey, KT6 7HT.
www.grosvenorhousepublishing.co.uk

This book is sold subject to the conditions that it shall not, by way of trade or otherwise, be lent, resold, hired out or otherwise circulated without the author's or publisher's prior consent in any form of binding or cover other than that in which it is published and without a similar condition including this condition being imposed on the subsequent purchaser.

A CIP record for this book
is available from the British Library

ISBN 978-1-80381-885-6

"An abundance mindset is like a
cookie jar that never empties.
No matter how many cookies you take,
there's always one more waiting!"

Ava A.S. Jacobs

Hey, Super Kids!

Did you know we're all kinds of amazing? Seriously – if we were a sandwich, we'd be the one with all your favourite fillings and none of the stuff you don't like. If we were superheroes, we'd be the ones who save the day when you think all hope is lost. That's how awesome we are!

I believe in us, and I mean REALLY believe. Like, 'believing that your favourite candy will magically appear when you want it' kind of belief. We've got this superpower to shape the future positively. Yup, you heard it right – we're time travellers!

Sometimes, even superheroes need a little nudge to awaken their powers. That's where I come in, hoping to light up that spark within us. Consider me your friendly neighbourhood 'Mini Mentor'.

You guys inspire me more than a triple rainbow after a summer rain. And I'm so grateful you trust me to guide you on this epic journey. Together, we'll transform those curious minds of ours into powerhouses that will make the world a better place.

So, let's buckle up, keep our snacks handy (because even superheroes get hungry), and set off on our quest. The future is waiting, and it's looking brighter already!

Your Mini Mentor,

Ava

Ava A.S. Jacobs

Contents

On: Abundance 1
On: Appearance 4
On: Calmness 7
On: Courage 10
On: Curiousness 13
On: Decluttering 16
On: Dreaming Big 19
On: Empathy 22
On: Facing Your Fears 25
On: Flow 28
On: Focus 31
On: Forgiving 34
On: Friendship 37
On: Generosity 40
On: Good Habits 43
On: Gratitude 46
On: Humility 49
On: Integrity 52
On: Kindness 55
On: Leadership 58
On: Learning 61
On: Listening 64
On: Manners 67
On: Moral Values 70
On: Morning Routines 73
On: Patience 76

On:	Peer Pressure	79
On:	Perseverance	82
On:	Positive Affirmations	85
On:	Positive Energy	88
On:	Positive Language	90
On:	Positive Thinking	93
On:	Procrastinating	96
On:	Reflection	99
On:	Reputation	102
On:	Respect	105
On:	Responsibility	108
On:	Rest and Sleep	111
On:	Sadness	114
On:	Self-Belief	117
On:	Selflessness	120
On:	Self-Love	123
On:	Setting Goals	126
On:	Standards	129
On:	Staying Healthy	132
On:	The Golden Rule	135
On:	The Law of Attraction	138
On:	Trustworthiness	141
On:	Visualisation	144
On:	Vulnerability	147

A Letter from Ava

First off, a massive high-five to you all for picking up this book! Trust me, you've just made a decision that's cooler than an ice cream on a hot summer day. I, Ava Jacobs, your Mini Mentor, want to send you a colossal THANK YOU for embarking on this journey with my book, *The Mini Mentor. The Power of Possibility: Short Stories to Inspire and Motivate Young Dreamers.*

Now, let's get down to business (the fun kind). You, young minds, are a powerhouse of endless imagination, creativity, and potential. Don't believe me? Just think about the last time you turned a cardboard box into a spaceship or a blanket fort into a castle. That's the magic of your mind at work! And guess what? There's no limit to it.

As you age, you might hear some folks say, "'that's impossible' or, 'you can't do that'. But keep in mind that these are the same people who likely forgot how they transformed a simple bath towel into a superhero cape when they were kids. So, hold on to that spark. Fan it, fuel it, and let it light the way to new adventures and possibilities.

This book is filled with transformative short stories designed to ignite that spark in your extraordinary young minds. Each level is a lesson, each lesson a stepping stone to greatness. Because you and I, my friends, are the future leaders, the innovators, the change-makers. The future is in our hands, quite literally, with this book.

Remember, the world is like a giant jigsaw puzzle. It's waiting for bright minds like ours to assemble the pieces, solve the mysteries, and make it a better place. So, let's roll up our sleeves (or cape if you're feeling particularly superhero-*ish* today) and dive headfirst into abundance and positivity.

Okay, budding superheroes, here's the final scoop!

Remember that every mind-blowing adventure starts with a single stride or a dramatic page flip. This guide is like an epic video game with 50 levels of knowledge. Why not tackle one level per week? That way, we'll conquer the entire game in a year and still have two weeks to celebrate our victory.

Replay each lesson like your favourite song. Mull over how to use the lesson and become a wisdom warrior, sharing knowledge like viral memes.

Oh, and, guess what? Each adventure we dive into comes with a mind-bending tongue twister, a 'Mega Monster Word' to add some extra zing! At the close of each story, we'll unravel the mystery behind these monster words. Our mission? To tame these words, become buddies with them, and invite them on our epic journey.

In conclusion, let us all be those cool stones that create waves of inspiration when tossed into the pond of life. Others will see those ripples and think, *Dude, I wanna make waves like that!* Are we ready to flip that page and launch our adventure? Game on!

Happy reading,

Ava A.S. Jacobs

On: Abundance

Once upon a time, in a world strikingly similar to ours yet with a dash of the extraordinary, lived an enchanting young girl named Becky. Becky was not your ordinary girl; she was a dreamer and a doer, with a dream as boundless as the endless sky. She had a simple yet profound wish – to sprinkle the world with sparkling dust, transforming it into a place brimming with joy and prosperity. But the question that perplexed her was, how? After much **contemplation**, she discovered the secret key – a complex concept for her tender age of ten – the 'abundance mindset'.

So, what is this abundance mindset? Imagine possessing an enchanted treasure chest that never runs out of precious jewels. It's about understanding that the world is bountiful, with enough goodies for everyone. It's about sharing our toys, snacks, or radiant smiles, filling voids, and bringing happiness. It's about having faith in our unique superpowers and stories instead of fretting over who has the most extravagant action figure collection.

On the contrary, the scarcity mindset, the polar opposite of abundance, is like a looming dark cloud of worry. It makes you feel insignificant and fearful, leading you to believe that if your friend triumphs in the school race, it somehow translates to your defeat. It's akin to a nerve-wracking game of musical chairs where the fear of losing your seat overshadows the joy of the game.

Becky embarked on her mission with a heart full of hope and a mind filled with determination. She wanted to introduce her friends, family, and anyone willing to listen to the magic of an abundance mindset. She taught them life wasn't a giant, stressful game of musical chairs. She taught them that everyone could have their generous slice of the cake without leaving anyone deprived. She guided them in discovering their inherent superpowers and demonstrated how this magical mindset could help them conquer the most formidable monsters in life.

As Becky started disseminating her magical lessons, they began to resonate with her loved ones. The word spread like wildfire and, soon enough, more and more people wanted to learn about this transformative abundance mindset. Becky was ecstatic, her heart swelling with joy! She could see her dream turning into reality. She was sprinkling her sparkle dust, making a difference in the world, one mindset at a time.

In no time, Becky's name echoed in every nook and corner as the little girl who taught the world to think abundantly. She knew this magical mindset would be instrumental in helping people accomplish their dreams and lead lives filled with happiness and success.

In the end, Becky's journey profoundly impacted not just her but everyone around her. She taught them that an abundance mindset was akin to a magic key. A key that unlocked limitless creativity fostered teamwork over the competition, celebrated our unique stories, and painted a future as bright and colourful as a rainbow gracing the sky after a summer rain.

And so, they all lived happily and abundantly ever after. Becky and her powerful abundance mindset transformed their lives, and the world became a better place.

The End.

Tongue Twister of this Story:

'Contemplation' – This is when you take some time to think really deeply about something. Imagine you're trying to decide what present to buy for your best mate's birthday. You might sit quietly, thinking about everything they like, what they already have, and what might make them the happiest. That's contemplation!

On: Appearance

Once upon a time, in the heart of a lively metropolis known as Sunville, there resided a spirited and radiant lass named Jenny. She was an energetic ten-year-old with sparkling sapphire eyes, a crown of unruly curls, and a smile that could outshine the sun. At a casual glance, Jenny might appear like any other child her age. She had a fondness for ice creams and a cheeky pet cat named Whiskers, and she relished her free time adventuring in the enchanted nooks of her garden. However, Jenny had an extraordinary quality – she had a natural flair for fashion and always looked impeccably stylish, regardless of the occasion.

Jenny belonged to an affluent family who could easily afford all the latest high-end fashion trends that were all the rage among the children in Sunville. But our unique little heroine, Jenny, had a taste of her own. She favoured simplicity with a dash of chic. Her style wasn't about flaunting flashy designer labels or donning ostentatious outfits; instead, she opted for clean-cut clothing with a sprinkle of pizzazz. Her signature look was a well-fitted pair of denim jeans coupled with a vibrant top, often accentuated by a quirky hairband or a pair of colourful socks.

Whenever Jenny gathered with her mates at the local park or the ice cream parlour, they couldn't help but admire how she looked so effortlessly stylish, even in her everyday clothes. For Jenny, it wasn't about the monetary value of her clothes but about paying attention to the minute details. Her shoes were always polished, her tops wrinkle-free, and her accessories matched perfectly. She had a gift for coordinating her clothes, crafting distinctive outfits that never failed to catch the eye.

Jenny's sharp eye for detail didn't just make her a budding fashionista; it also assisted her to excel in other aspects of her life. From securing top grades in school with her neat and colourful projects to arranging the most enjoyable play dates with her friends, Jenny's **meticulous** approach was hard to overlook. Jenny's impeccable style was always noticed whether she was at the grocery store with her mum, selecting the ripest fruits, or grabbing a quick snack with her friends at the local sandwich shop.

Special occasions, like parties or school events, Jenny viewed as an opportunity to showcase her fashion sense while maintaining her elegance. She would invest time in selecting her outfit, ensuring it was suitable for the occasion and reflected her distinctive style. Her sophisticated and refined fashion sense – quite remarkable for a girl her age – always earned her admiration, all thanks to her smart dressing.

Jenny's story reminds us that one doesn't need pricey labels to make a fashion statement. All it requires is a bit of dedication and mindfulness about what one wears. Keeping up with trends can be fun, but moderation is key.

Remember to stay true to your style, just like Jenny did. Looking neat and tidy sends a powerful message about self-esteem and pride in oneself. So, dress smart, think smart, and confidently live your life! And most importantly, let your personality shine through your style, just like our stylish little protagonist, Jenny.

Thus, they lived stylishly ever after, with Jenny leading the way with her exceptional style and infectious enthusiasm for life.

The End.

Tongue Twister of this Story:

'Meticulous' – Imagine if you're colouring a picture and you make sure to stay inside the lines. Or maybe when you tidy your room and put each toy back precisely where it belongs. When you take your time to do something very carefully and pay lots of attention to every little detail, that's what we call being 'meticulous'. It's like being super careful and precise!

On: Calmness

Once upon a time, two best friends lived side by side in a snug little corner of the world known as Friendship Town. Their names were Tommy and Sally. They were as close as two peas in a pod, their bond stronger than the strongest oak tree. You could always find them together – whether they were playing a lively game of tag in the park, their giggles ringing through the rustling leaves, sharing scrumptious sandwiches on bright, sunny picnic days, crumbs dancing around them as their chatter filled the air, or tackling tricky homework assignments, their room filled with the scratch-scratch-scratch of their pencils.

One day, a test, as big and intimidating as a looming mountain, cast its shadow over their usually sunny world. Tommy felt a whirlwind of worry brewing inside him, a storm threatening to shatter his confidence. He knew he had to gather all his courage, summon all his knowledge, and give it his best shot to conquer this mountainous task.

As the test day arrived, Tommy was a jumble of nerves, trembling like a leaf caught in a gusty wind. But Sally, who always radiated calmness even during the most turbulent times, reminded him to take deep, soothing breaths before stepping into the arena of tricky questions. She encouraged him to stay cool as a cucumber, no matter how twisty and turny the questions might be.

Tommy took her advice to heart, each word deeply ingrained in his mind. He did his utmost during the test, wrestling each question with sheer determination.

But when the test ended, he was left in a sea of uncertainty. He didn't know if he had conquered the mountain or stumbled down its rocky slopes. He couldn't shake off the nagging feeling of disappointment because things hadn't unfolded as he had imagined.

When he returned home, things deteriorated when Sally, with her heartwarming smile, asked Tommy how the test had gone. He exploded like a dormant volcano, spewing out his frustration and anger about how things hadn't gone according to his plans.

Sally was taken aback; she had never seen Tommy lose his cool like this. It was like watching a serene lake suddenly transform into a **tempestuous** ocean. After a moment of stunned silence, she gently said, "I understand you're upset right now, but remember, our friendship is stronger than any difficult day at school."

Tommy instantly realised he had let his emotions run wild. He apologised for his fiery outburst and cooled down by taking a few more deep, calming breaths. He felt as if a heavy burden had been lifted off his shoulders.

From that day forward, he solemnly promised never to let his emotions cloud his judgement or affect his friendships. He understood that it's okay to feel disappointed when things don't go as planned, but staying calm, composed, and kind-hearted is essential if we want our friendships to thrive through all life's ups and downs.

And so they lived happily, learning and growing every day after that. They encountered more tests and challenges, but their bond remained unbroken, their friendship shining as a beacon of hope in the face of adversity.

The End.

Tongue Twister of this Story:

'Tempestuous' – Imagine a really stormy day when the wind is howling, and the rain is lashing down. Everything outside seems wild and rowdy. Well, when something or someone is 'tempestuous', it means they're just like that storm – wild, energetic, and maybe a bit unpredictable!

On: Courage

Once upon a time, a delightful little hamlet existed under the gentle caress of a sunbeam-kissed morning brimming with the promise of thrilling escapades. This hamlet, cosily nestled between imposing hills and a glistening creek, was a serene oasis, blissfully cocooned from the frenzy and tumult of the outside world. An imaginative ten-year-old boy, known as Timmy, lived in this peaceful sanctuary.

Timmy was a captivating boy whose vibrant dreams and fanciful stories were the talk of the hamlet. Yet, despite his colourful imagination, he often shied away from challenges. Be it a daring pursuit in the woods or a mundane household task, Timmy's **apprehensions** loomed over him like relentless shadows, whispering words of doubt into his ears.

On this particular sunbeam-kissed day, the serenity of the hamlet was disrupted by whispers of an impending grand tournament. The whispers travelled from one doorstep to another, amplifying and becoming more contagious with each passing moment. Stories of a magical award bestowed by the king himself began to circulate, filling the air with a palpable sense of anticipation. This prospect caused Timmy's heart to flutter with a mix of exhilaration and apprehension. Here was his golden chance to demonstrate his bravery to his friends, family, and, indeed, the whole world!

Yet, as Timmy considered entering the tournament, a frigid wave of fear swept over him, chilling his determination. He agonised over the possibility of faltering during the competition, the ensuing laughter that might ring out, and the crushing disappointment of not achieving victory. But after several sleepless nights wrestling with his fears, he mustered his inner fortitude and decided to confront his fears. His hand trembled as he signed up for the tournament, but his heart was resolute.

The day of the tournament arrived, bathed in a clear, radiant light that stirred up a symphony of emotions within Timmy. He was a bundle of nerves, his stomach twisting into knots. Yet beneath the layer of anxiety, a spark of resolve flickered that refused to be quenched. He strode to the village square, shoulders back and chin up, vowing not to let fear intimidate him.

The tournament was a formidable test of intellect, strength, and mettle. It stretched Timmy to his limits, challenging him in ways he had never experienced before. But with every obstacle he overcame, his courage swelled, becoming stronger and more steadfast. To his immense surprise and joy, he found himself standing in the final round – and then, he emerged victorious! The king himself presented Timmy with a golden medal, his eyes shimmering with admiration for the young boy's bravery.

That day, Timmy discovered that courage wasn't just about tournaments and competitions. It was a superpower that could guide him through the turbulent seas of life. For instance, when a complex lesson left him puzzled back in school, he noticed others were also confused but too afraid to ask. He raised his hand with newfound bravery and confessed he didn't understand. His courage sparked a discussion on the topic that enlightened the entire class.

From that day on, Timmy became a shining beacon of bravery, inspiring others with his remarkable courage. Whether it was a significant task or a minor one, he tackled each with equal vigour. He realised that courage was the magic feather that could help him soar towards success. If he allowed fear to clip his wings, he might never reach the heights he was capable of.

And so, dear young ones, this enchanting story of Timmy imparts a valuable lesson: courage is our secret armour. It empowers us to explore new frontiers unfettered by the chains of fear.

The End.

Tongue Twister of this Story:

'Apprehensions' – If you have apprehensions about something, you're worried or scared about what might happen. It's like when you're nervous before your first day at a new school because you're unsure how things will go. That feeling of being sceptical and nervous is called 'apprehension'.

On: Curiousness

Once upon a time, nestled in a world strikingly similar to ours, lived a young girl named Molly. Molly was an effervescent sprite, brimming with a thirst for knowledge and an **insatiable** curiosity as infinite as the cosmos. Every sunrise heralded a fresh adventure waiting to be unravelled; every tick of the clock was a compelling mystery begging to be solved. Her eyes, aglow with fascination, twinkled more brightly than the northernmost star as she pondered the enigmas of the universe surrounding her.

On a particularly enchanting day, when the sun set, the heavens ablaze with a dazzling display of gold and orange, Molly resolved to undertake an audacious expedition. She made a courageous vow: she would savour cuisine from every nook and cranny of the globe! From the fiery depths of Indian biryani that set her palate ablaze in a fiery dance to the succulent Chinese dumplings that exploded with an orchestra of flavours and the exotic African okra stew that sang a melody unlike any other – Molly relished them all.

Through these gastronomic adventures, Molly unearthed something remarkable. Novel experiences were not fearsome dragons lurking in the shadows but hidden treasure troves overflowing with unforeseen delights, waiting to be discovered by intrepid explorers.

Spurred on by this insight, Molly vowed to seize every opportunity that fluttered her way, much like a determined butterfly pursuing the sun's warm embrace. She travelled to remote lands far beyond her quaint hometown, from the teeming metropolises of Japan, where neon lights pirouetted in the darkness, to the awe-inspiring mountains of Peru, where ancient secrets murmured in the breeze. In each location, she tasted every unusual dish, each morsel a new entry in her ever-expanding chronicle of adventures.

However, Molly's curiosity was a relentless creature that refused to be satiated by merely tasting the world – she yearned to experience all it had to offer! She dared herself to scale towering cliffs, leaving no stone unexplored. She plunged into the labyrinth of Mandarin language lessons, unravelling the complex maze of a foreign dialect. She even joined a book club teeming with an eclectic mix of individuals from all walks of life. Through these experiences, she grew to appreciate the vibrant tapestry of cultures and viewpoints that colour our world, an invaluable lesson for a budding explorer.

Molly's daring curiosity was a magical key that opened up a universe of adventures, yet she knew that not everyone was as eager to veer off the beaten track. Some people favoured the comforting cocoon of their daily routines, apprehensive about dipping their toes into the refreshing waters of the unknown. But Molly believed a pinch of curiosity was necessary to avoid missing out on life's magic.

From Molly's perspective, curiosity was not merely a characteristic but a guiding light – the key that unlocked personal growth, the compass that directed towards understanding, and the spark that ignited evolution. Without exploration, we remain oblivious to the miracles of the world around us, and without sampling new experiences, we stagnate in a sea of missed opportunities.

Molly's story serves as a shining beacon, a lighthouse in the vast ocean of life, reminding us that we should never fear stepping beyond our comfort zones. Cultivating our curiosity is akin to nurturing a magical beanstalk; one never knows how tall it might grow or what wonders await at its zenith!

So, as we close the chapter on Molly's story, remember that it's not the end, but rather, just the beginning. The world is a canvas teeming with boundless adventures, waiting for curious explorers like you to adorn it with your unique hues. So venture forth and explore, for who knows what marvels await you!

The End.

Tongue Twister of this Story:

'Insatiable' – Imagine you really love ice cream, and no matter how much you eat, you still want more. You never seem to get enough of it. That's what 'insatiable' means – when you want more and more of something and are never completely satisfied or full.

On: Decluttering

Once upon a time, on a bright and beautiful morning when the sunbeams danced merrily on dew-kissed leaves, there lived an adventurous lad named Johnny. He had sparkling eyes full of curiosity and a heart that held a deep affection for all things unusual and charming. Every nook and cranny he explored, every dusty corner and hidden alleyway he found would reveal something unique, something he could add to his ever-growing collection of treasures. These ranged from ancient books whispering stories of distant lands to toys glittering like stardust, from vibrant clothes fresher than a rainbow's palette to ornaments murmuring stories of times long past. Johnny cherished each find.

Initially, this peculiar hobby was an exhilarating adventure, a treasure hunt that filled his heart with joy and his eyes with wonder. His room evolved into a mystical museum, bursting at the seams with curiosities. But as days rolled into weeks and weeks blended into months, his once snug haven began to resemble a disorderly jungle. Mountains of items towered over him, making Johnny feel like a minute mouse lost in a maze of cheese. Despite his best efforts to organise the chaos, it seemed impossible, akin to squeezing a giant into a teacup.

One day, as the sun streamed through the clutter, Johnny had an epiphany. His beloved collections, the treasures he had painstakingly gathered, were transforming into troublesome obstacles. They cast long, **ominous** shadows over his sunny disposition, morphing his cheer into gloom. The clutter started to play tricks on his mind, turning him from a cheerful lad into a grumpy gnome. Johnny realised he needed to brandish the magic wand of decluttering to conquer the chaos and restore his room to its former tranquil glory.

When Johnny felt daunted by the enormity of the task, his faithful band of friends rallied around him like knights charging in to save the day. They spun enthralling stories of how decluttering could elevate spirits and sprinkle positivity like fairy dust. They warned him about the sly beast named Hoarding that lurked in the shadows, ready to snatch away joy and peace. They encouraged him to retain only what was genuinely precious and necessary and to bid farewell to the rest.

His friends revealed secret strategies for decluttering, wisdom woven into practical advice. They suggested donating items no longer needed or finding someone who would treasure his surplus trinkets. Emboldened by their support, Johnny began to shed layers of his collections, just like peeling an onion, revealing a cleaner, calmer space beneath.

As he cleared the clutter, Johnny felt as light and free as a bird soaring high in the sky. Unexpected benefits began to appear like delightful surprises. He could now find his favourite comic book without having to dig through a mountain of stuff! But the most magical transformation occurred within Johnny himself. He discovered that releasing certain items brought more joy, satisfaction, and tranquillity than hoarding them ever had.

So, here's the golden nugget from Johnny's story, a pearl of wisdom for you all: decluttering can sprinkle magic dust on our lives, simplifying things and making us happier and brighter! Don't be afraid to say goodbye to things you don't need anymore. Remember, giving away can be as thrilling and rewarding as acquiring something new!

And so, with hearts lighter and rooms tidier, they all lived happily ever after.

The End.

Tongue Twister of this Story:

'Ominous' – This is a word we use to describe something that makes you feel like something bad is going to happen. It's like seeing dark clouds in the sky and thinking it will storm soon. So, if something feels or looks 'ominous', it feels or looks like it might not be very nice or could cause trouble.

On: Dreaming Big

Once upon a time, beneath the star-studded canopy of the night sky in a world not unlike ours, there lived a spirited young lass named Jasmine. This world was infused with its own special magic, and Jasmine, with her heart aflame with boundless dreams, was its radiant beacon. There was something extraordinary about Jasmine; she was a daydreamer, her dreams as limitless and unending as the universe. She yearned to see these dreams become reality, yet often found herself lost in a labyrinth of thoughts, wondering how to make her dreams come alive.

One day, a shadow of disappointment descended over Jasmine's usually bright spirits. On this day, destiny led her to cross paths with an elderly, wise man famed for his enchanting stories about the beauty and mystery of dreaming big. His words swirled around her like sparks from a roaring campfire, igniting a spark of curiosity within her.

The old sage explained to Jasmine that dreaming big wasn't just about **concocting** fanciful dreams. It was about realising that even she, who seemed like an ordinary girl, possessed the power to create extraordinary things if she dared to believe in her capabilities. He guided her gently towards setting ambitious goals, goals that made her heart flutter with pure excitement.

He assured her that with a sprinkle of courage, a touch of determination, and a generous amount of persistence, even the goals that seemed as distant as the farthest stars could be within her reach.

He encouraged Jasmine to step outside her comfort zone because she could uncover her hidden potential only by venturing into the unknown.

The sage then shared a secret as vital as the air we breathe. He confided in Jasmine, saying, "Remember, my dear, you are unique and special. If your mind can visualise and believe it, you can achieve it. So, dream BIG – for there is nothing to lose."

Jasmine's heart swelled with anticipation, her eyes shining brighter than the celestial constellations in the sky above. She promised to heed his advice and reach for the stars and galaxies far beyond.

Jasmine began her journey with renewed courage, realising that the path to success was strewn with bumps and falls. She understood that these mishaps, or 'hiccups' as she playfully referred to them, were merely stepping stones towards triumph. If you never stumble, then perhaps your dreams aren't grand enough! The finish line can't be crossed without a few trips and tumbles.

Whenever Jasmine felt the tendrils of surrender creeping up on her or found herself daunted by the monumental task ahead, she would remember the sage's wise advice: dream big and do not fear failure.

Powered by his wisdom and her newfound bravery, Jasmine dived headfirst into achieving her daring dreams. Days slipped into weeks, weeks into months, and months into years, and slowly but surely, her wildest dreams transformed from mere figments of her imagination into a beautiful reality she lived and breathed every day.

And so, Jasmine and her dreams lived happily ever after, inspiring others to dream big and believe in themselves.

The End.

Tongue Twister of this Story:

'Concocting' – Imagine you're in the kitchen with all sorts of ingredients like flour, sugar, eggs, and butter. You decide to mix them all in a bowl, maybe add some chocolate chips too, and then bake them in the oven. What comes out? A delicious cookie! That's what 'concocting' means – mixing different things to create something new and interesting, just like you did with the ingredients to make your cookie.

On: Empathy

Once upon a time, a young maiden named Lily lived in a picturesque town cradled amidst rolling emerald hills and glistening brooks. Her heart was as soft as the petals of a freshly bloomed daisy and as vast as the sparkling night sky. She admired every living being, from the minuscule ant, marching diligently, to the majestic elephant, lumbering gracefully. Lily was a ray of sunshine in her little hamlet, always ready to lend a helping hand, transforming even the toughest of trials into golden opportunities with her kindness and understanding.

What set Lily apart wasn't some extraordinary capability to fly or become invisible but something far more remarkable. Lily was bestowed with the magical ability of empathy. This enchanting gift allowed her to step into others' shoes, experience their world, and genuinely comprehend their emotions, dreams, and tribulations.

Lily recognised that this power of empathy wasn't merely a personal trait but a tool she could wield to spread joy and unity in her community. Like a fairy dusting stardust, she used her empathy to sprinkle happiness and tranquillity wherever she journeyed.

So, what is empathy? Imagine this scenario: your best mate has misplaced his cherished toy, and you can feel his devastation as if it were your own. Or, visualise comprehending why your sibling gets upset when you borrow their belongings without asking.

That's empathy. It allows us to connect with other people's feelings without letting our personal **biases** cloud our judgment.

Why is empathy so important? Empathy bridges divisions, cultivate understanding, and advance harmony. It enables us to form authentic bonds, comprehend others' viewpoints, and find mutual ground rather than fuel disagreements.

Empathy is a gentle nudge of the power of kindness, a virtue that seems to be dwindling in today's fast-paced world. An empathetic person can forge formidable relationships and make our world more secure and joyful. When individuals feel acknowledged and understood, they are more likely to seek assistance when required.

Intriguingly, empathy also serves as a mirror, reflecting our own feelings and reactions. By empathising with others, we can better identify and comprehend our own emotions and biases that might obstruct us from forming genuine bonds.

How can we foster the power of empathy like Lily? The initial step is active listening. When someone is speaking, please give them your complete attention without preparing a response or passing judgment. Allow them to narrate their story in its entirety without interruptions.

Next, practice stepping into their shoes. Before making decisions or starting conversations, consider their viewpoint. This nurtures understanding and aids in establishing deeper connections rather than abrupt reactions.

Remember, a world devoid of empathy resembles a garden bereft of blossoms. It can result in misunderstandings and conflicts, escalating situations due to poor or non-existent communication.

So, let's endeavour to mirror Lily's empathy today. Let's display more empathy towards everyone around us – those close to our hearts and those residing thousands of miles away. After all, empathy is a superpower that enhances the quality of life for everyone, fostering a world where everyone feels seen, heard, and understood.

The End.

Tongue Twister of this Story:

'Biases' – You know how sometimes when you're choosing between two things, like maybe chocolate and vanilla ice cream, and you really, really like chocolate more than vanilla, so you always pick chocolate? That's a bit like what 'biases' means. It's when we prefer one thing over another, not because it's better or right but just because we like it more for some reason. Sometimes, this can be unfair, especially when dealing with people. So, trying not to let our biases make decisions for us is essential.

On: Facing Your Fears

Once upon a time, a ten-year-old wonder named Maria lived in a world as vivid as a child's imagination. Maria wasn't just your everyday girl; she was an adventurer at heart, exploring the vast landscapes of her life with an insatiable curiosity. Yet, like many young explorers, she carried an unusual backpack. It wasn't filled with toys or books but with a medley of fears that would often creep out, catching her off guard.

Sometimes, it was the sight of a spider spinning its delicate web in a forgotten corner of her room or the daunting prospect of speaking aloud in front of her classmates. These fears felt like colossal mountains, casting long, ominous shadows over her spirit. They were so overwhelming that there were days when Maria wished to stay cocooned in her snug bed, safely distanced from the world and her dreams.

However, Maria was not one to back down easily; she was a warrior at heart. She believed that within her lay a roar of courage as mighty as a lion's, waiting for the right moment to unleash itself.

One bright and sunny morning, as golden rays of sunlight streamed through her window, Maria made a decision that would change her life forever. She decided it was time to face the monsters hiding in the shadows of her fears. Sitting at her small wooden desk, she penned all her fears on a pristine sheet of paper, resolving to confront them one by one.

First on her list was the fear of spiders. Instead of shying away, Maria chose to learn more about these intriguing creatures. She immersed herself in captivating documentaries, marvelling at how they spun their intricate webs and kept the natural balance by preying on pesky insects. The more she discovered, the less terrifying they appeared. When she next encountered a spider, she didn't flee in fear; instead, she observed, enchanted by the elegance of its web.

Next, Maria decided to conquer her fear of public speaking. She bravely enrolled in speech classes at school and spent countless hours engrossed in books about effective communication. Every sentence she spoke, every page she turned, made her feel more confident and resilient. Before long, she was not just surviving presentations but genuinely enjoying them, transforming what was once a fear into an exhilarating challenge!

Feeling **invigorated** by her victories, Maria decided to step further outside her comfort zone. She donned a chef's hat and whipped up scrumptious dishes; she twirled gracefully in dance lessons and even joined the school sports team, kicking the football with renewed vigour. Activities that once filled her heart with dread now made it flutter with joy and anticipation.

With each fear Maria faced, she grew happier and more fulfilled. She realised that the only limitations were the ones she set for herself. She was becoming braver than she ever thought possible, fearlessly embracing the unknown and feeling ready to conquer the world.

Maria's journey inspired all who knew her, showcasing the immense power of facing one's fears.

She felt like she had scaled a mountain of fears, standing triumphant and proud at its peak. Deep down, she knew that if she could overcome her fears, indeed, nothing was impossible!

And so, Maria continued her journey, courageously overcoming whatever came her way, becoming a living testament to the power of bravery. And in this world of everyday adventures, they all lived happily ever after.

The End.

Tongue Twister of this Story:

'Invigorated' – Imagine you're feeling exhausted after a long day of playing, and then you have a nice rest, eat a yummy dinner, and suddenly you feel full of energy again, ready to play some more. That's what 'invigorated' means – it's like a recharge for your body or mind, making you feel strong and full of life again!

On: Flow

Once upon a time, a boy named Jack lived in the heart of a bustling town. Jack was not your average youngster. He had an amazing knack for constructing marvellous things from ordinary materials. Like you, his mind was a curiosity and imagination treasure trove.

Each day was a thrilling quest for him, a golden opportunity to turn his wildest dreams into reality. He made miniature boats to sail in his bathtub, intricate bridges that spanned from one corner of his bedroom to the other, and even grand castles built entirely from colourful blocks. But his most splendid creation? A small robot that could move around and engage in conversation!

However, Jack faced a seemingly impossible challenge. Despite his love for crafting these impressive creations, he struggled to remain committed to a single project for extended periods. He often became fidgety, his mind drifting away to other thoughts, leaving his brilliant inventions incomplete.

On a magical day, as if by fate, Jack stumbled upon an ancient book on a concept called 'flow'. Its pages were tinged with the patina of age. The book described 'flow' as a state where you become so engrossed in an activity you adore that it feels as though the rest of the world has faded away. It's just you and your exciting project in your own little universe.

Intrigued by this idea, Jack decided to try this 'flow' thing out. He devoted his attention solely to projects that ignited his joy and challenged his abilities. After several weeks of consistent practice, Jack started entering the 'flow' more naturally than ever before.

But that wasn't all. Jack didn't just find it easier to stay focused; he also observed several other wonderful transformations. His building pace quickened, his ideas became more inventive, and sometimes, he'd astonish himself with the complexity of his creations. And the icing on the cake? He found that taking brief breaks from his projects helped refresh his mind, enabling him to tackle any obstacles with a **rejuvenated** perspective when he resumed
his work.

For Jack, being in 'flow' meant immersing himself entirely into his passion: creating. This journey imparted a valuable lesson to him. When you pour your heart and soul into activities that fill you with joy, it spreads positivity to all aspects of your life. Your motivation soars high, your skills fine-tune swiftly, and you'll always be satisfied regardless of the final outcome.

So here's the grand moral: if you want to experience authentic happiness in any activity you undertake, ensure it puts you in the 'flow', whether you're eight, ten, 13, or any age.

The End.

Tongue Twister of this Story:
'Rejuvenated' – Imagine if you have a really old, tired teddy bear, and one day, you give it a good wash, sew up any tears,

and fluff up its stuffing. Suddenly, your teddy bear looks almost new again, as if it's just had a long, refreshing sleep. That's what 'rejuvenated' means – it's when something old or tired is made to look or feel fresh and lively again.

On: Focus

Once upon a time, a spirited young boy named Sam lived in a nearby realm just a whisper beyond reality. This boy's imagination was a boundless universe, brimming with dreams as vast as the infinite heavens, and his heart was a treasure trove of bravery and courage. However, our daring Sam often was embroiled in a web of difficulties. Much like a butterfly fluttering from bloom to bloom, he would flit from one thrilling escapade to another, never quite managing to see them through to their conclusion.

One radiant afternoon, bathed in the sun's golden glow, he found himself deep in conversation with his parents. They shared a secret with him, their voices filled with love and their eyes sparkling with wisdom. "Sam," they murmured gently, "always remember this – wherever your focus goes, your energy flows!" This simple yet profound phrase ignited a flame within Sam's curious eyes. He resolved that from then on he would concentrate on one exhilarating adventure at a time and channel all his boundless energy into seeing it through to its triumphant end.

To master this new strategy, Sam began with small tasks perfectly matched to his capabilities. Gradually, with patience as **steadfast** as a rock and determination as fierce as a lion, he honed the art of maintaining laser-like focus. Every time he accomplished a task, a surge of exhilaration swept over him, making him feel as light and free as a bird soaring high in the cerulean skies. His energy seemed inexhaustible, propelling him to take on even larger challenges that had previously appeared as daunting as towering giants.

Throughout this journey, Sam unravelled the enchanting charm of focus. He realised that by pouring all his energy into a single endeavour at a time, he could attain victories more splendidly than if he attempted to balance multiple tasks simultaneously. The reward wasn't just about completing things quicker or better, but also the exhilarating feeling of accomplishment that made him feel invincible, akin to a superhero. This sense of achievement can fuel our inner strength, particularly when the path ahead appears steep and arduous.

With this potent secret safely planted in his heart, Sam evolved into an intrepid explorer who never baulked at a challenge. No matter how towering the mountain or how deep the ocean, he would remind himself 'where focus goes, energy flows', and bravely continue his journey. Taking on one project or quest at a time, Sam conquered feats that were once mere figments of his vibrant imagination.

So, my dear young friends, remember that no matter how sky-high your dreams may be, tackle them one step at a time. Wherever focus goes, energy flows!

And thus, Sam, his parents, and all who heard his story, lived their lives with unwavering focus and determination, leading to many joyous and fulfilling conclusions.

The End.

Tongue Twister of this Story:

'Steadfast' – It simply means to be very determined or unchanging in your purpose. Imagine if you're trying to learn to ride a bike, and even if you fall off a few times, you keep getting back on and trying again because you really want to learn – that's being 'steadfast'. You're sticking to your goal no matter what happens.

On: Forgiving

Once upon a time, in a land not too far away, there existed two steadfast chums, Jack and Sarah. They were as inseparable as two halves of the same biscuit, their friendship as snug as a pair of gloves on a frosty winter's day.

Their bond was unshakeable, and they did everything together. From scaling towering trees to uncovering hidden caverns, their companionship was second to none. Every day was brimming with chuckles and shared secrets, making them feel like two peas in the same cosy pod.

However, a misunderstanding overshadowed their radiant friendship on one bright and sunny day. A tiff sprouted between them, transforming their usually warm chats into icy exchanges. Jack's pride felt punctured, akin to an abruptly burst balloon, while Sarah felt like a puppy that had accidentally gnawed on a cherished slipper but was too afraid to confess.

Days morphed into weeks, and the atmosphere between them fizzed with tension, similar to a sweater charged with static. The once jubilant playground now seemed gloomy, their joint jokes and laughter replaced by uncomfortable silences and fleeting glances.

But Sarah, with courage comparable to a lioness safeguarding her young, decided to thaw the frosty situation. She approached Jack with a gentle voice. "Jack, our friendship is caught in a storm, but if we don't learn to forgive, we'll never sail back to sunnier shores."

Sarah's words **reverberated** in Jack's mind, bouncing about like a ball in a pinball machine. He knew she was spot-on, but the memory of their dispute still smarted like stepping on a bee during a barefoot summer day. Sarah peered at him with wide, sincere eyes. "What if I made a mistake? Wouldn't you want to forgive me?" For Jack, it was an epiphany, a sudden realisation. Nobody's flawless, and everyone stumbles on their shoelaces occasionally. We should be prepared to extend the same courtesy if we anticipate others to forgive us when we falter.

Taking a long breath, Jack expressed his willingness to forgive Sarah. It wouldn't be a simple task, but they both needed to empathise with each other and acknowledge their roles in the disagreement, no matter how minuscule.

Sarah nodded her understanding, appreciative of Jack's decision to let go of his grudge. From that point forward, they made an effort to communicate more candidly and forgive more readily when encountering bumps on their journey. Their friendship sparkled brighter than ever, like a rainbow adorning the sky after a storm.

So, dear friends, here's a golden piece of wisdom from Jack and Sarah's story: even when the path gets bumpy with your pals, forgiveness is the magic potion that can weave you closer than ever, like a cosy blanket on a chilly winter night.

With newfound maturity and comprehension, they continued on their shared adventure. They lived joyously, learning more about each other, growing together, and fortifying their friendship daily, like a tree gaining strength with each passing season. And to this day, their story of friendship and forgiveness continues.

The End.

Tongue Twister of this Story:

'Reverberated' – Imagine you're in a big room or a hall, and you shout, "Hello!" You'll hear your own voice come back to you, right? That's because your voice bounces off the walls and returns to you. This bouncing back of sound is what we call 'reverberated'. So, when a sound is 'reverberated', it means it's echoing or bouncing back.

On: Friendship

Once upon a time, an energetic young girl named Amy lived in a land not so far away, nestled between shimmering emerald hills and fields of golden sunflowers. She was akin to a fledgling bird, ready to spread her wings and embark on her first flight. The world of school, vast and unchartered, lay before her, filling her heart with a blend of excitement and apprehension. The prospect of making new friends thrilled her, yet the mystery of who her best friends would be had left her a tad nervous.

In these moments of uncertainty, Amy remembered the sage words of her beloved granny. "Show me your friends, and I'll show you who you are." This phrase, intriguing and **enigmatic**, stirred her curiosity. What could it possibly mean?

With a spirit of determination and the heart of an explorer, Amy set out to unravel this riddle. Her quest led her to seek companions who shared her interests – the magical worlds hidden within the pages of books, the vibrant kaleidoscope of colours in art, and the rhythmic melodies of music that made her heart sway. The journey had its challenges and stumbling blocks, but Amy persevered. Eventually, she found a splendid group of friends whose passions resonated with hers. Their camaraderie infused her school life with courage and joy, turning every day into a delightful escapade.

These newfound friends radiated kindness, a quality Amy deeply admired. Their infectious warmth gradually transformed her into a more considerate and compassionate individual. They spurred her to unfurl her wings and evolve into the best version of herself rather than dragging her into an abyss of negativity.

As the days rolled into weeks, Amy discovered the phenomenal power of true friendship. Her friends were like superheroes, always ready to swoop in and save the day during challenging times, or lend a hand with perplexing school projects. Their friendship was a sturdy bridge that strengthened each day, making Amy feel part of an extraordinary tribe within the school.

But just as every story has villains, the school world is no different. Amy quickly realised that associating with the wrong crowd could lead to mischief and chaos. Getting trapped in the spider's web of trouble was too easy due to peer pressure.

However, in this journey of friendships, Amy learned that being a good friend was just as crucial as having one. As the age-old adage goes, a friend in need is a friend in deed – a superhero cloaked in disguise.

So, remember, dear friends, keep Granny's wise words close to your heart, like a compass guiding you through life's labyrinth. Surround yourself with positive and uplifting friends, and you'll witness first-hand how her timeless advice – 'show me your friends, and I'll show you who you are' – can powerfully shape your identity from a tender age.

And so it unfolded: in the companionship of her true friends, Amy navigated the tumultuous waves of school life. Together, they laughed, learned, and grew, living out their own version of 'happily ever after'.

The End.

Tongue Twister of this Story:

'Enigmatic' – Imagine you've got a puzzle box that's difficult to open because it has many secret compartments and hidden latches. You're unsure how to solve it; it's a bit of a mystery. That's what 'enigmatic' means. It's used to describe something or someone that's a bit puzzling or mysterious because they're not easy to understand.

On: Generosity

Once upon a time, camaraderie and community thrived in the heart of a picturesque village tucked amidst rolling emerald hills. Among its inhabitants was an exuberant and spirited young boy named Jack. His family resided in a quaint, humble home, their means modest, with limited resources. Jack's heart was filled with empathy for his hardworking parents, and he yearned to alleviate their struggles. Yet he found himself at a standstill, unsure how to translate his earnest desire into tangible action.

On a fine, sunlit day, under the sprawling branches of a grand old oak, Jack chanced upon a conversation between two elderly villagers. They spoke with a hint of sorrow about individuals too engrossed in their own lives, unaware of the needs of their fellow villagers. Their words resonated with Jack. The idea of generosity transforming the world into a haven of happiness sparked a flame within him. He resolved to sprinkle this magic of kindness throughout his community, one thoughtful act at a time.

So began Jack's noble quest. He became a familiar sight around the village, assisting neighbours with heavy water pails, clearing away branches fallen from storm-ravaged trees, and engaging the younger children in fascinating games, offering their weary parents a well-deserved break. Jack painted a vivid picture of selfless giving through these simple acts, demonstrating that true generosity expects no rewards. His deeds of compassion echoed through the hearts of his fellow villagers, and whispers of his kindness began to ripple across the community.

As the seasons changed, Jack's generosity shone brightly, a beacon of warmth and selflessness. His actions ignited a chain of **reciprocity** amongst the villagers. Reciprocity is like when you lend your favourite book to a friend, and they lend you theirs in return. It's a wonderful give-and-take where both parties do something kind for each other. It's all about fairness and treating others as you would like to be treated. The once sparse cupboards in Jack's home gradually overflowed with food parcels and tokens of gratitude from the neighbours; a testament to his care for their children.

Jack unravelled a precious lesson through this heart-warming journey: sharing is truly the most beautiful form of caring! Generosity isn't about neglecting one's own needs but recognising that we are all intertwined in the grand tapestry of life. Kindness and respect can create a vibrant community spirit, enriching everyone's lives.

Jack's story is a timeless testament to the power of generosity, one kind act at a time.

And so, dear children, let our story end here with a reminder that even the smallest act of kindness can make a big difference.

The End.

Tongue Twister of this Story:

'Reciprocity' – Let's say you share your toys with your friend today, and tomorrow they share their toys with you. That's called 'reciprocity'. It's like an unspoken rule of being fair and kind to each other. So, if you do something nice for someone, they'll do something nice for you in return. That's reciprocity!

On: Good Habits

Once upon a time, a young girl named Anna lived in a quaint little town that was not so different from yours or mine. She was a whirlwind of joy and energy, smiling as bright as the morning sun and laughter that rang through the narrow lanes. However, this lively sprite also had an uncanny knack for finding herself in a pickle. Whether it was forgetting her homework, arriving fashionably late at gatherings, or letting her fiery temper get the better of her when things didn't go her way, Anna was a tornado of mischief. Her parents watched with furrowed brows, their worry growing like a shadow at dusk, pondering how these habits could shape her future.

One sunny afternoon, Anna's mum took it upon herself to demystify the enigma of habits for her daughter. She painted habits as unseen puppet masters, subtly choreographing the dance of our lives. Good habits, like diligently brushing your teeth every morning or finishing your homework promptly, are your loyal comrades, illuminating the road towards your dreams. In contrast, bad habits, such as munching on too many sweets, spending hours glued to a screen, or staying up past bedtime, act like cunning jesters, steering you away from being the best version of yourself.

Anna absorbed her mother's wisdom, but a knot of apprehension coiled in her stomach. How was she to break free from these **unyielding** bad habits? Sensing her daughter's dilemma, her mum proposed starting with small, manageable steps. Instead of attempting a giant leap, Anna could aim for minor victories each day, like dedicating 15 minutes to losing herself in the pages of an enchanting book rather than staring at a screen, or exploring yummy yet healthy smoothie recipes instead of succumbing to sugary indulgences.

To make this journey more enjoyable, a reward system could be introduced. Like a scoop of her favourite ice cream, a small treat could be her reward for conquering the daunting essay lurking in her school bag. The pièce de résistance of this self-improvement journey would be 'reflection'. At the end of each week, Anna should retreat into a quiet corner and reflect on her progress, celebrating her victories and strategising how to tackle any obstacles that tripped her up.

Embracing these principles was no easy feat for Anna. But her fiery determination refused to be dampened, and her unwavering commitment stood strong like a sturdy oak. Slowly but surely, like a seasoned detective, she began to discern between the habits of her allies and those of her adversaries. Armed with this newfound wisdom, she bid farewell to detrimental habits and welcomed more beneficial ones.

So, our little heroine embarked on her journey of self-improvement, cultivating one good habit at a time and gradually transforming herself into the best version she could possibly be.

And they lived happily ever after.

The End.

Tongue Twister of this Story:

'Unyielding' – Imagine your favourite superhero who never gives up, no matter how tough things get. They keep going and never let anything stop them. That's what 'unyielding' means – not giving up or not changing, even when things are really hard.

On: Gratitude

Once upon a time, in a world where the sky was crystal blue, and the sea was a shimmering quilt of turquoise, there lived a tiny turtle named Toby. Toby was an extraordinary young creature with a heart as deep and expansive as the ocean he called his home, and dreams as countless as the grains of sand that carpeted the seashore. Yet, despite being blessed with bountiful seaweed snacks and all the warm sunbeams he could ever wish to bask in, Toby often withdrew into his shell, preoccupied with the dreams that hadn't yet blossomed.

On one magical day, Grandpa Ripple, the most ancient sage turtle in the entire ocean, swam over to Toby. Grandpa Ripple had braved many tempests and witnessed countless sunrises; his shell was adorned with the marks of time and wisdom. He had heard about Toby's concerns and decided it was time to share a profound piece of wisdom about the power of gratitude. "Dearest Toby," he began, his voice as soothing as the gentle lullaby of the waves, "gratitude isn't about yearning for more marvels. It's about cherishing the marvels we're already surrounded by!"

He urged the little turtle to look around his aquatic kingdom and count each blessing, from the twinkling sea stars that adorned the ocean's ceiling to the silky sand beneath his petite flippers. He encouraged Toby to listen to the harmonious songs of the whales, to feel the rhythmic dance of the ocean currents, and to savour the tangy saltiness that pervaded their underwater home.

Inspired by Grandpa Ripple's wisdom, Toby started to weave gratitude into his everyday life. Whenever a vibrant fish whizzed past or a colourful coral flourished, he chuckled with gratitude. Whenever a surprise shower of seashells rained down on his path, he hooted with heartfelt thanks. Soon, he found himself brimming with joy as bubbly and **effervescent** as the ocean foam, even when the sea grew a tad dark or the currents slightly powerful.

Every day, Toby thanked the great ocean for all the aquatic gifts he received and sought strength during turbulent tides and challenging twists. Even when his plans were swept away like ephemeral sea foam, he never forgot to express his gratitude for the present moment. This newfound 'attitude of gratitude' served as a lighthouse, guiding him through the darkest depths and lighting up even the most intimidating deep-sea plunges.

Toby's story is a glowing reminder that gratitude can illuminate our lives, regardless of our circumstances. It helps us recognise the magic in every moment, whether big or small, and navigate life's whirlpools with a heart brimming with hope. Gratitude is like a treasure map, revealing how wealthy we truly are, even when the journey becomes perilous.

So, my dear young friends, whenever you find yourself trapped in a vortex of worries, remember our friend, Toby, and his profound mantra: maintain an attitude of gratitude! Regardless of the storms we encounter, embracing gratitude can transform our lives into an eternal adventure.

And so, they lived happily ever after.

The End.

Tongue Twister of this Story:

'Effervescent' – Imagine opening a bottle of fizzy drink like lemonade. Do you see all those tiny bubbles popping up and dancing around? That's what 'effervescent' means. It's bubbly, lively, and energetic, just like those bubbles!

On: Humility

Once upon a time, in a kingdom far beyond the reach of ordinary maps, a young boy named Prince Oliver resided in an enormous castle, its towers piercing the sky. Oliver was just a sprout of ten summers old and was blessed with all the luxuries a boy his age could ever dream of. His chambers were adorned with the most extraordinary playthings from across the globe, and a team of royal chefs stood ready to bake his beloved triple chocolate cake at a moment's notice.

However, despite the overflowing wealth and privileges, young Oliver often found himself gazing out of the castle's grand windows, lost in thought. He had all the material possessions one could desire, yet true happiness seemed like a shy bird that always flew away.

One fine day, Oliver decided he'd had enough of his golden prison. He swapped his diamond-encrusted royal carriage and plush velvet robes for a pair of well-worn trainers and plain attire. With a heart brimming with resolve and a backpack hanging on his shoulder, he embarked on an adventure to find the elusive piece of his happiness jigsaw.

As Oliver journeyed through quaint villages and bustling towns, he encountered simple folks who didn't reside in towering castles or wear glittering gold crowns. Yet, their laughter was more contagious, and their smiles sparkled brighter than the largest gem in his treasure trove. This perplexed the young prince. "How can they be so joyous with so little?" he pondered, scratching his royal head in **bewilderment**.

Then he stumbled upon something magical. These humble folk shared whatever little they possessed without hesitation. They lent a hand during tough times and celebrated each other's victories with genuine joy. There was no trace of jealousy or malice in their hearts. Instead, they held a treasure much more precious than gold or jewels. They were rich in the golden virtue of humility!

Prince Oliver learned that humility wasn't about owning a colossal castle or the most gleaming crown. It was about prioritising others, cherishing the small joys, and never being too proud to seek help. It was about sharing your last biscuit, even if your belly grumbled in protest!

With these revelations lighting up his mind, Oliver realised that while his treasure chest was brimming with riches, his heart was as barren as a desert. He resolved to change this and filled his heart with the golden treasure of humility. True, he wouldn't be the wealthiest or the most famous, but he would certainly be the happiest. And, after all, isn't happiness the greatest treasure of all?

Upon his return to the kingdom, he left his ego at the castle gates. He shared his toys with the children of his realm, asked his royal chefs to cook a grand feast for everyone, and even exchanged his golden crown for a simple cap. His once solemn castle now resonated with laughter and cheerful chatter, and his heart overflowed with bliss.

Ultimately, our little Prince Oliver discovered that while power could rule kingdoms, humility could win hearts. And isn't ruling hearts far more rewarding? So, as we say goodbye to our wise little prince, let us remember his lesson: in the game of life, it's not power but humility that truly triumphs. It's not about who crosses the finish line first but who touches the most hearts along their journey.

And with that, we close our storybook on Prince Oliver, who taught us that humility isn't merely a virtue; it's a superpower.

The End.

Tongue Twister of this Story:

'Bewilderment' – Imagine walking into a room and finding everything upside down – the chairs, the tables, even your favourite toys! You'd be really confused, wouldn't you? You wouldn't know why it happened or what to do next. That feeling of being very confused and not knowing what is going on is called 'bewilderment'.

On: Integrity

Once upon a time, in a quaint little village nestled amidst towering mountains and lush green meadows, there lived a boy. His name was Ian, and though he wasn't the tallest or the strongest, he was indeed mighty. His might didn't come from physical strength but from a virtue he possessed – honesty! This attribute earned him the affectionate nickname 'Honest Ian', making him as sought after in the village as ice cream on a sweltering summer's day.

When Ian was just a wee lad, his parents instilled in him the value of integrity. They often told him, "Integrity, dear Ian, is like your invisible superhero cape. It's all about doing the right thing, even when it feels as challenging as eating broccoli or finishing your homework on a Saturday night!"

Ian absorbed these wise words like a sponge, adorning his integrity like a shiny superhero badge. He was consistently truthful, even if it meant confessing that he had snaffled the last cookie – yes, even the much-loved chocolate chip ones! He respected everyone's views, even if they expressed something as peculiar as pineapple being a suitable topping for pizza. His integrity made him a trusted figure in the village, as reliable as a robust tree branch during a climbing competition.

Whenever the villagers needed assistance or guidance, they'd scamper to Ian quicker than a squirrel sprinting after its prized acorn. And why, you wonder? Because they knew Honest Ian would always tell it straight, without any **sugarcoating**. His unwavering integrity made him as popular as the swings during recess. His friends valued his honesty, adults applauded his sense of responsibility, and even the grumpiest grandmas, who could be as sour as pickles, were charmed by his sincerity.

But what if one forgets their integrity, much like forgetting an umbrella on a rainy day? Well, people might start sidestepping you as they would a pile of stinky dog mess. Your friends may lose faith in your words, supervisors may question your work, and your loved ones might start to doubt if they can depend on you, much like doubting a wobbly chair's ability to support them.

The most exciting part? Everyone has the potential to be a superhero of integrity! You can strengthen your integrity muscles bit by bit, just like constructing a towering Lego masterpiece. Here are some tips:

1. Speak up – Be courageous and stand for what's right, even if it feels as uncomfortable as standing barefoot on squishy, slimy worms.
2. Respect others – Value everyone's opinions as if they were rare jewels, even if they seem as odd as socks on a chicken (I mean, who's ever seen a chicken wearing socks?).
3. Keep your promises – If you say you'll do something, stick to it! No 'buts' or 'maybes'. It's like a secret handshake of trust.

4. Apologise when you're wrong – We all make mistakes! Saying sorry shows you're maturing, not just growing taller.
5. Be open-minded – Keep your mind receptive to new ideas, like a mouth ready for a massive, tasty burger.

Ian became the emblem of integrity in his village, garnering respect from all, from tiniest tots to toothless old-timers. And remember, every superhero has a secret weapon; Ian's was his unwavering integrity! He wore it proudly, demonstrating to everyone that being honest, genuine, and true to oneself is the most powerful superpower anyone can possess.

And so, the villagers lived honestly ever after, their lives enriched by the lessons of integrity imparted by our superhero, Honest Ian.

The End.

Tongue Twister of this Story:

'Sugarcoating' – This is a term we use when someone tells a story or gives information in a way that makes it seem nicer or less harsh than it really is. Just like when you coat or cover something with sugar to make it taste sweet, 'sugarcoating' is when someone tries to make something that might be unpleasant or difficult to hear easier to accept. It's like if you had to take a bitter medicine and your mum put a bit of honey on the spoon to make it taste better. That's what we call 'sugarcoating'.

On: Kindness

Once upon a time, in a realm beyond where the rainbow ends, there lay a charming little hamlet known as Kindville. Kindville was more than merely a geographical location; it was an emotion akin to the warmth of a snuggly hug on a frosty winter's day. It was a mystical place where every person beamed with a smile as radiant as a glimmering gem and harboured a heart overflowing with love. And what is the secret ingredient that sparked this magic? A dash of potent kindness!

In the mesmerising world of Kindville, the villagers regarded kindness not as an optional add-on to life but as an essential element, as vital as oxygen for survival. They revered kindness, letting it billow in the breeze like a superhero's flowing cape, boldly declaring their extraordinary power. They realised that embodying kindness was more profound than merely making others feel joyous – it was their covert weapon to metamorphose the world into a utopia.

Every morning in Kindville started with bright sunshine that painted the sky with hopeful colours. When the sun rose and spread its golden light over everything, the villagers would wonder, *What kind thing can I do today?* Every new day was a thrilling adventure filled with endless opportunities to spread the amazing power of kindness.

The young inhabitants of Kindville were initiated into the powers of kindness even before they mastered the art of tying their shoelaces. They were taught that kindness functioned like a boomerang – the more you flung it out into the universe, the more it whirled back to you. They found out that being kind made forging friendships simpler than triumphing at a game of noughts and crosses, and it was the secret spice in the recipe to untangle any dilemma, no matter how tangled it seemed.

However, in Kindville, kindness wasn't merely a present for others. It also served as a nurturing **elixir** for one's own spirit. Every villager knew that when they executed a kind act, it ignited a warm and fuzzy sensation within them, as soothing as sipping hot cocoa on a nippy winter day. And earning the title of a kind child in Kindville made you as popular as the town's confectionery shop teeming with delicious sweets!

But, like every story, Kindville had its share of baddies. Some folks didn't value the magic of being kind. They thought it was as useful as a chocolate kettle, melting at the first sign of trouble. They believed that kindness was a sign of weakness and that if you did something wrong, you could escape punishment because others would be too kind to tell you off. But what they needed to understand was real kindness isn't about letting people off the hook; it's about understanding, forgiving, and helping each other to grow.

Despite the few souls who misinterpreted the true essence, Kindville was a sanctuary of kindness. It stood lofty and proud, a luminous beacon to the wider world, demonstrating that we're all connected by unseen threads of affection and empathy. And that, dear readers, is the genuine power of kindness.

Thus, the saga of Kindville endures, eternally disseminating its message like ripples in a lake. Kindness isn't merely a virtue; it's a superpower capable of revolutionising the world!

And with this, our story concludes, but bear in mind that the magic of kindness perpetuates forever and always in every heart and every deed.

The End.

Tongue Twister of this Story:

'Elixir' – This is a bit like a magical potion. Imagine if you were playing a video game and you found a special drink that could make your character stronger, healthier, or even give them special powers – that's kind of what an elixir is. In real life, people sometimes call medicines or other things that are meant to improve your health 'elixirs'. But remember, in real life, not all potions or 'elixirs' you might hear about actually work, so it's always important to listen to doctors and grown-ups about what is safe to take!

On: Leadership

Once upon a time, a young lad named Charlie lived in a vibrant town buzzing with life and laughter. Now, Charlie wasn't just any ordinary boy. His dreams were as vast as the sky, towering higher than the loftiest ice cream cone you've ever seen! He yearned for more than just being Charlie; he aspired to be a leader, a victor, and a hero. The captivating stories of legendary leaders who could ignite sparks in people's hearts like countless twinkling fireflies had often filled his ears. And every time, he would wonder, *Why not me? Why can't I be the one to inspire joy and instil bravery?*

With a heart brimming with resolve and a rucksack packed with curiosity, Charlie embarked on a remarkable adventure to unravel the hidden recipe of leadership. He plunged into enchanting books overflowing with stories of **valiant** leaders who overcame fears and accomplished the unimaginable. He held animated discussions with his mates in the playground, who were already captaining their own exciting imaginary pirate crews or superhero squads.

On his journey, Charlie stumbled upon an astonishing truth. Leadership wasn't about donning a glistening crown or bellowing orders with a thunderous voice. Absolutely not! It was about understanding his friends' dreams, listening to their fantastical ideas, and offering a comforting shoulder when they stumbled over their shoelaces.

Charlie discovered that the most extraordinary leaders weren't the ones who stood aloft but those who bent down to tie a friend's undone shoe. They were the brave souls who dared to venture into the unknown before others, always prepared to lend a hand to help their comrades cross the petrifying monster-infested river. They were the ones who remembered where the treasure was buried, ensured everyone got a slice of the birthday cake, confessed when they thought broccoli tasted like rubbery greens, and upheld their belief in the existence of unicorns and superheroes.

Gradually, Charlie transformed from a dreamer to an achiever, from a lad to a mini-hero. He set heartening examples for his friends by helping them untangle their knotty problems. He even started doing extra chores at home, astonishing his parents as they didn't even have to ask!

With a dash of perseverance that danced in his eyes, a spoonful of patience sweeter than treacle, and a hefty serving of determination as solid as a chocolate chip in a biscuit, Charlie began evolving into an incredible super-leader. Before he knew it, he found himself encircled by a squad of friends who admired his leadership skills and appreciated his assistance.

Charlie's exciting journey into leadership taught him some nifty tricks. He learned to empathise with others' feelings as if they were his own, bounce back from a botched science experiment with a grin, respect adults (even when they insisted vanilla was a superior ice cream flavour to chocolate), collaborate to build the loftiest sandcastle, console a friend who lost their favourite toy, and solve mysteries such as the vanishing of the last biscuit.

By practising these leadership skills early in life, Charlie built enough confidence to face any fire-breathing dragon, scale any towering mountain, or even complete his tricky maths homework on time.

So, dear mates, remember, just like Charlie, you too can be a leader. All it takes is a little courage that roars like a lion, a lot of kindness that blossoms like a sunflower, and an endless supply of imagination that soars across galaxies. So go forth, commence your adventure, and become the protagonist of your story.

And they all lived happily ever after.

The End.

Tongue Twister of this Story:

'Valiant' – This is a fancy word to describe a very brave and courageous person. Imagine a knight in shiny armour, standing tall and fearless, ready to protect his kingdom from a dragon. That knight is being valiant. He's not scared, even though he might face something big and scary. So, when you're being strong and brave, even when something seems tough or scary, you're being valiant!

On: Learning

Once upon a time, an enthusiastic girl named Ana resided in a realm where imagination and reality danced together. Her eyes twinkled with a brightness that could put the stars to shame, and her mind was a bustling hive of inquisitive bees, ever-hungry for knowledge. Ana's parents watched her curiosity
bloom with delight, like seeing a sunflower unfurling towards the morning sun.

Ana's inquiry knew no bounds as she questioned everything from the blueness of the sky to the emotional power of music. Upon discovering answers, the joy that lit up her eyes was like a grand spectacle of fireworks illuminating the night sky. Encouraged by this, her parents, her biggest cheerleaders, urged her to excel in school and always complete her homework – as essential to her as a superhero's cape.

As the seasons changed, Ana realised that learning was nothing short of magical, turning ordinary days into thrilling adventures filled with discoveries. She learned that if she delved into her books with the courage of a fearless adventurer, even the most complex concepts would reveal themselves like hidden treasures in a mystical forest. Learning new skills, such as playing a guitar or speaking another language, felt like finding secret keys that could open unseen doors, leading to unimaginable future escapades.

Learning evolved into Ana's superpower, which she cherished and nurtured like a precious, magical stone. She understood that the more effort she put into her studies today, the stronger her superpower would become, readying her to face tomorrow's mythical beasts and daring challenges.

Ana soared high above the clouds in school, becoming one of the shining knights of knowledge in her realm. She aced every test and project, her scores gleaming brighter than the North Star. Her classmates admired her not just for her intelligence but also for her unwavering perseverance. They saw her dedication to always staying a step ahead, so when high school became a complex maze, she had already mastered the map and was ready with her compass.

When it was time for her to embark on the grand journey to university, Ana's commitment to learning turned into golden acceptance scrolls from the most **prestigious** institutions across the kingdom. Yet, Ana's thirst for knowledge remained unquenched, like a desert yearning for rain. She savoured learning, seeing it not just as a route to academic or career success but also as the secret ingredient in crafting a life brimming with joy, fulfilment, and endless awe.

Life continually offers us glittering opportunities to learn and evolve, much like hidden gems waiting to be unearthed. It's our responsibility to grab these golden chances. As our heroine, Ana, demonstrated, a passion for learning is a magical key that unlocks infinite doors leading to exhilarating adventures and boundless possibilities, both now and in the future!

And so, our story concludes! But remember, every ending is merely a new beginning, and your learning adventure has just begun!

The End.

Tongue Twister of this Story:

'Prestigious' – This is a big word that means something or someone is very well-known and respected. It's like when your favourite footballer wins the 'player of the year' award; they become prestigious because many people admire them. Or if you win first place in the school spelling bee, that's prestigious because you worked hard and did better than everyone else!

On: Listening

Once upon a time, a house humming with warmth, love and laughter stood in the heart of a snug and cheerful neighbourhood. This was the home of an effervescent little girl named Sarah, who had sparkling eyes full of dreams and a curious mind. Like any child her age, Sarah treasured her parents dearly, trusting them to guide her through life's meandering paths. Yet, like all children, Sarah had her moments of mischief and disobedience.

Sometimes, her parents would request her help around the house or remind her not to indulge in too many cookies before dinner, but Sarah often pretended she hadn't heard them. She'd play by her own rules, brushing aside their words of wisdom. However, this habit was soon to change.

One sunny afternoon, after Sarah had conveniently 'overlooked' her mum's request to set the table for lunch, her mother thought it was time for a meaningful conversation. With a smile as warm as a summer's day, she beckoned Sarah to join her on the plush living room sofa. "My darling," she began, her tone soft yet resolute, "your dad and I only want what's best for you. Even if it seems like we're being a bit strict sometimes."

Sarah's curiosity was stirred as she looked at her mum. Her mother carried on, "We understand that making mistakes is part of growing up, but by listening to us, you can avoid some of the stumbling blocks we've encountered."

Sarah listened intently as her mother explained how being attentive could help her avoid future troubles, especially when navigating the world independently. She learned how listening could transform their home into a haven of peace, devoid of conflicts and filled with mutual understanding.

This conversation left a profound impression on Sarah. From that day forward, she vowed to pay attention to her parents' tender advice. It was a challenging transformation, but Sarah was resolute.

As the days evolved into months and the months matured into years, Sarah blossomed into a young lady. She realised the invaluable benefits of listening to those who truly cared for her – particularly her parents. Listening morphed into her superpower! She cultivated her skill to discern between helpful advice and unnecessary noise.

By applying her parents' nuggets of wisdom, Sarah excelled in school, work, and at home. She sidestepped the pitfalls they had once tripped over and evaded the errors they had committed. Undeniably, comprehending why certain things were the way they were wasn't always a cakewalk. Yet, thanks to the solid bridge of trust established over the years, Sarah could fondly **reminisce** about her childhood days when this invaluable lesson moulded her into the radiant beacon she had become.

One thing remained clear: listening was the secret recipe for a contented life and a harmonious household. The more they listened to one another, the less they squabbled, filling their home with sunshine and heart-warming smiles!

And so they continued to live happily ever after, listening, learning, and laughing together. But be sure to remember, dear young friends, that Sarah's listening superpower can also be yours – all it requires is your willingness to lend an attentive ear.

The End.

Tongue Twister of this Story:

'Reminisce' – This is when you think back to fun times or special moments that have happened in the past. Imagine if you've had a really fun day at the seaside, and later, when you're back home, you start to remember how much fun you had building sandcastles, eating ice cream, and splashing in the water. That's called reminiscing – it's like replaying happy memories in your mind, almost like watching your favourite film again!

On: Manners

Once upon a time, a young lad named Tommy lived in a town that could have been just about anywhere. Tommy wasn't your run-of-the-mill boy, oh no. He was a special kind of chap, known far and wide for his politeness that was as extraordinary as a superhero's powers. But instead of a cape or a mask, Tommy's superpower was his impeccable manners.

Tommy was the sort of lad who would swing open doors with such style for anyone coming along behind him. He liberally sprinkled 'please' and 'thank you' like magical stardust at every turn, treating everyone with such immense respect that it seemed as if he carried a bottomless bucket of it wherever he went.

His mum and dad were brimming with pride for their polite little gentleman. They strutted around town like proud peacocks flaunting a gleaming new feather. At every town gathering, they sang his praises as if he was a local hero. Even his mates, who would sometimes poke harmless fun at his courteous ways behind his back, couldn't help but admire him.

One bright and sunny day, Tommy's parents decided to reward him with a special treat. They took him to a posh restaurant – the kind where the menu seemed like it was written in **hieroglyphics**. But Tommy, our polite hero, didn't bat an eyelid. He walked in as quietly as a ninja on a top-secret mission, spoke softly as if sharing confidential knowledge, sat as straight as a castle tower, and always ensured everyone else was sorted before he helped himself. His exceptional behaviour was like a lighthouse beacon, drawing everyone's eyes towards him. Even the usually distant waiter gave him an approving nod.

As Tommy grew older, he realised that his super-manners weren't just for show; they had real power! His politeness and kindness seemed to cast a spell on people, making them want to be nicer, too. And the most magical part? By treating others with respect, he earned their respect in return. His manners were like a golden ticket, helping him make friends and succeed in life.

But here's the tricky bit. Good manners are not just about knowing which cutlery to use at dinner or how to hold doors for others properly. It's also about understanding other people's feelings. For instance, not playing your music loud on the bus or doing silly dances in inappropriate places. Small gestures like these can say a lot about a person. And let's not forget about chewing with your mouth closed at meal times!

Good manners become your unique signature, a shiny emblem that helps you stand out from the crowd. Teachers love well-behaved students who can cooperate with others, and bosses value polite employees who can work well in a team. Having good manners is like having your very own cheerleading squad!

So, my young listeners, the moral of this story is that top-notch manners are incredibly important in life. They're not just fancy words or polite actions; they're your superpower. Good manners help you earn the trust and respect of those around you. When you treat everyone kindly, expecting nothing in return, you can feel good about yourself – perhaps even feel like you're on top of the world!

So, my future stars, here's the secret recipe. If you want to shine like a rare gem now and in the future, keep practising your best behaviour whenever possible. And remember, every superhero needs their superpower, so make yours good manners!

And with that, we bring our story to a close!

The End.

Tongue Twister of this Story:

'Hieroglyphics' – These are a bit like secret codes or special pictures that people in ancient Egypt used as writing a long time ago. Instead of letters and words, as we use now, they would draw symbols or little pictures to tell stories or send messages. So, if you ever see a picture of an eye, a bird, or a strange symbol on an old Egyptian wall or piece of paper, you're looking at hieroglyphics!

On: Moral Values

Once upon a time, in an era where the sun painted golden streaks across the azure sky, nestled a town abuzz with the vibrant energy of its young inhabitants. This place was home to an extraordinary group of children, a band of lively little explorers, each heart brimming with an insatiable curiosity. They embarked on a grand expedition to decode the enigma they'd overheard the adults discussing – the profound concept of moral values.

Armed with their innocent curiosity, these mini-detectives sought the wisdom of every parent, teacher, and grandparent within their reach. The answers they received were as diverse and colourful as the hues that danced across the sky after a refreshing summer shower. This enigma, a riddle swaddled in mystery, only served to fuel their determination.

These moral values they sought are like unseen magic wands, the kind you encounter in enchanting fairy stories. These values illuminate our path through life's labyrinth, casting a gentle glow to guide us. They're akin to the secret ingredients in Granny's cherished recipe that make it so delectable. These virtues – honesty, integrity, respect, kindness, fairness, and compassion – are our superpowers, which we wield to spread goodness, creating a happier world.

As they delved further into their mission, these **audacious** youngsters realised the numerous advantages of possessing these superpowers.

It was like having a magnet for friendships, drawing trust and camaraderie from those around them.
It was akin to having a brain equipped with a built-in compass, always pointing towards the right decisions. And, it was like brewing a special concoction that helped forge friendships as robust and steadfast as a castle, rooted in respect and understanding.

But what if, they wondered, one day, you lost your magic wand, misplaced your secret ingredients, or forgot where you stashed your superpowers? Oh no! That's when you might find yourself lost in life's maze, making choices that induce a frown and struggling to build friendships. Who would want to be in such a pickle?

As the sun journeyed across the sky, our young explorers realised that the earlier they flexed these moral muscles, the stronger they'd become. Just like training for the annual sports day at school, these values could help them sprint ahead in life, both on the playground and later in the grand game of life.

With their determined eyes sparkling like distant galaxies, they made a solemn pact under the setting sun. They vowed to become the superheroes of their narratives, living with bravery and integrity regardless of life's unexpected twists and turns.

As the sun bid farewell, their day of discovery concluded. But their voyage was only just commencing. Each step reverberated with the promise of a future steeped in kindness, honesty, and respect as they strolled home.

And so, their lives were not just filled with joy and laughter. They lived with purpose and valiantly, scattering goodness wherever their paths led. And that, my dear young friends, is the most splendid 'happily ever after' anyone could ever hope for.

The End.

Tongue Twister of this Story:

'Audacious' – This is a big word that describes someone brave and daring, but in a cheeky or bold way. Imagine if one of your mates decided to sing a song in front of the whole school during assembly, even though they were told not to. That would be pretty audacious! It's like having the courage to do something that might surprise or shock people because it's so unexpected.

On: Morning Routines

Once upon a time, in the bustling heart of a lively town known as Springsville, a beaming 10-year-old girl named Claire resided. Claire was no ordinary girl; she was an effervescent burst of energy, with dreams as towering as the loftiest skyscrapers and as radiant as a gleaming summer's day. She cherished school more than she loved her ice cream sundaes, and if you knew the depth of her affection for those sugary delights, you'd understand that's quite a significant statement!

However, poor Claire was entangled in a whirlwind of tasks each morning. Her mornings were less of a tranquil sunrise and more akin to a frantic dash against the relentless ticking of the clock. This daily scramble often left her feeling deflated, like a balloon that had lost its bounce before she even set foot in her beloved school.

One fateful day, while her pencil was pirouetting across her notebook, forming doodles of all shapes and sizes, a sage old phrase from her mum suddenly sprang into her mind. *A good day begins with a good morning, darling.* Her mum would always utter these words, so Claire decided to take this golden piece of wisdom to heart and devise an extraordinary, out-of-this-world morning routine.

The following day, Claire leapt out of bed a half-hour earlier than usual as though she had springs attached to her feet. She picked up her favourite book and snuggled back under the warmth of her cosy blanket. There's nothing quite like starting the day with an enchanting story of heroes and villains. After plunging into her book for about ten minutes, she hopped out from under her blanket and did some amusing stretches and star jumps. She was aware that a bit of exercise not only shook off the drowsiness but also painted a colossal grin on her face.

After brushing her teeth until they gleamed like precious diamonds and donning her school uniform, Claire made sure to have a scrumptious, healthy breakfast. Her parents reminded her, "Breakfast is the brain's fuel, darling. Don't neglect to fill up!" Savouring every mouthful, she knew she was fuelling her brain for the thrilling day ahead.

And would you believe it? Claire completed all this with time to spare! She realised that having a morning routine was akin to possessing a secret weapon or a magical talisman. It prepared her for anything the day could throw her way, from unexpected maths quizzes to **impromptu** presentations.

Claire adhered to her morning routine as loyally as a knight vows allegiance to his king. It became a positive habit. She observed that she arrived at school each day feeling like a superheroine, ready to conquer whatever challenges came her way.

When report card day arrived, Claire's grades had soared! Her focus and alertness during class were unmatched. Furthermore, she was happier and more upbeat every day, demonstrating that a good morning routine was indeed the key to a fantastic day!

Claire learned that irrespective of the magnitude of the challenge, having a routine, big or small, can set you up for success – and that means your success, too. It's never too early to commence your morning routine because every superhero needs their secret weapon!

And so, Claire continued to flourish, her mornings no longer a whirlwind but a harmonious symphony. Each day was an adventure, every challenge an opportunity to shine.

The End.

Tongue Twister of this Story:

'Impromptu' - This means something you haven't planned or prepared for; it just happens suddenly. It's like when you're playing in the park and suddenly decide to start a football game with your friends. You didn't plan it before you left home; it just happened – that's an impromptu football game. It's all about doing things spontaneously, without any planning ahead.

On: Patience

Once upon a time, in the heart of a town as lively and colourful as a grand carnival, lived an exuberant little boy called Timmy. Imagine a bottle of sparkling lemonade, on the brink of overflowing with bubbles at the slightest joggle – that was our young friend, Timmy! A packet of limitless energy, ceaselessly on the go and forever in pursuit of the next escapade. Whether whizzing down the road on his gleaming crimson bicycle or munching his breakfast cornflakes like a ravenous bear, Timmy did everything at such a pace that would make even a cheetah green with envy.

On one particularly dazzling day, with the sun casting down its warm, golden glow, Timmy's mum decided it was an ideal day for some quality mother-son time. They embarked on a journey to the park, but this was not just any park; it was a paradise for children brimming with joyous swings, thrilling slides, and a cheerful ice cream stand that made Timmy's taste buds perform a jig of anticipation.

As soon as their shoes grazed the park entrance, Timmy's eyes lit up as they spotted the ice cream stand. His heart thumped with exhilaration, and he was all geared up to dash towards it, ready to dive into a luscious heap of creamy ice cream. But his mum, as sage as an owl, gently restrained him. "Hold your horses, Timmy," she said. "We'll enjoy an ice cream, but only after we've relished the park. You need to master the art of patience."

Timmy's face wrinkled in bewilderment, much like a piece of paper crumpled in vexation. Wait? This idea was as foreign to him as the extraterrestrials in his favourite comic books. Seeing his puzzled expression, his mum took a deep breath and elucidated the virtue of patience.

Envision patience as a superpower, a clandestine weapon in your life's toolbox. It's the ability to remain cool as a cucumber when things don't materialise with a simple flick of your fingers. Patience equips you with the might to make wiser decisions and prevents you from becoming a cranky, grumbling bear.

Sporting patience is akin to wearing a superhero's cape. It fosters stronger friendships, reduces stress levels, and unlocks a compassionate understanding of others. It's like having a magical key opening a treasure chest with invaluable benefits.

For instance, patience implies you can endure a long queue at the pizza parlour without drumming your fingers impatiently or lend an ear to your friend's lengthy story about their pet hamster without brusquely interrupting.

On the flip side, lacking patience is like wandering around with a gloomy thundercloud hovering above your head. It leads to unjustly accusing others for your mistakes, making rash decisions that could land you in a soup, and feeling more frustrated than a cat chasing its own tail.

As the day at the park gradually faded, Timmy's mum gently reminded him of the superpower of patience before they finally made their way to the ice cream stand. As he relished each lick of his long-awaited treat, he realised that the wait had made it taste even more divine!

Since that enlightening day, Timmy began to exercise his patience muscles more often. He discovered that life was significantly more delightful when you weren't constantly racing towards the finish line.

Thus, Timmy **metamorphosed** into a champion of patience, demonstrating that even the most energetic amongst us can learn to take things slow and steady.

And consequently, they lived happily, tranquilly, and patiently ever after.

The End.

Tongue Twister of this Story:

'Metamorphosed' - This is a big word that means something has changed a lot. Imagine if you drew a picture and then used your coloured pencils to change it completely – it would have metamorphosed! A good example is a caterpillar turning into a butterfly. That's a huge change. So, we say the caterpillar has 'metamorphosed' into a butterfly.

On: Peer Pressure

Once upon a time, in the enchanting twilight of a moon-kissed evening, nestled among undulating hills and flourishing meadows, you would find the delightful village of Littlefoot. This cosy nook of the world was home to a spirited young lass named Lily. She was as steadfast as a sunflower in the sun's warm embrace and as courageous as a noble knight donned in gleaming armour. The villagers were amiable souls, each with their own unique quirks and differences.

Every afternoon, as the school bell pealed through the valley, Lily and her band of friends, a cheerful group of pranksters, would congregate under the ancient oak tree at the heart of the park. They'd chatter incessantly, laugh uproariously, and play energetically while sharing stories of their daily adventures.

On one such sun-drenched afternoon, a friend leaned in **conspiratorially**, her eyes sparkling with the thrill of revelation. She whispered about a covert plan devised by the 'cool' kids. An audacious adventure was underfoot – a plunge into the river that wound through their quaint village. This river was shrouded in mystery and folklore; no one really knew whether swimming there was permitted or if it was just an alluring myth propagated by the older children.

The secret plan sent waves of exhilaration through the group. Everyone yearned to be part of this daring escapade, to secure their place in the 'cool' brigade. Lily felt the same pull, the invisible cords of peer pressure tugging at her. The allure of fun was enticing, even though a small voice within her cautioned that it might not be the most prudent decision.

The mere notion of opposing her friends stirred a tempest of butterflies in Lily's stomach. But our valiant heroine summoned all her courage and decided to stand against the current. Gathering all the strength she could muster, she voiced her concerns. "No, I don't think this is a good idea," she declared, her voice quivering slightly but her eyes ablaze with resolve. There were gasps of astonishment and looks of disbelief, but Lily stood her ground as unyielding as a boulder against the relentless surge of the sea.

As fate would have it, the river proved to be perilous. If Lily had succumbed to peer pressure, she could have plunged into a potentially catastrophic situation. This highlights the importance of resisting peer pressure, even when fear makes your knees tremble like a leaf in the wind.

Standing up to peer pressure is akin to donning a superhero's cape – a testament to your strength and bravery. It not only shields you from potential harm but also earns you the admiration of others. When you carve your own path instead of mindlessly following the crowd, people begin to see the glimmer of a leader in you.

The best part? Standing up against peer pressure bolsters your self-esteem. It reassures you that you are capable of making the right choices, even difficult ones. So remember, channel your inner Lily – stand tall against peer pressure, embrace bravery, and define your own version of 'cool'!

And so, they lived happily ever after.

The End.

Tongue Twister of this Story:

'Conspiratorially' – This is a word that describes when people are secretly planning something together, usually something naughty or mischievous. Imagine if you and your mates whisper together to plan a surprise birthday party for your teacher without her knowing – that's doing something conspiratorially!

On: Perseverance

Once upon a time, in a town that might very well be just like yours, there lived a young lad brimming with a ceaseless longing for knowledge. His name was John, but his friends fondly dubbed him 'Brainy Johnny', for his love for learning exceeded even his affection for ice cream sundaes – and let me assure you, he adored his ice cream sundaes!

But our Brainy Johnny had a potent secret weapon, a superpower that rendered him undefeatable, no matter the circumstances. And it wasn't something as mundane as flying or invisibility. Oh no! It was far more extraordinary than that. It was the power of perseverance!

Now, I hear you questioning, "Perseverance? That's not a superpower!" But let me assure you, my young explorers, perseverance is the most fantastic power one can possess.

Imagine having a superpower that propels you forward, regardless of how gruelling the journey becomes. It's akin to being a valiant knight in gleaming armour, facing down a fire-breathing
dragon, and defiantly yelling, "Bring it on!"

The magic of perseverance lies in its ability to morph problems into intriguing puzzles and formidable challenges into exhilarating games. It grants you the resilience to proclaim, "I can do this!" even when the task appears as monumental as a mountain. Moreover, it instils a superhero-like confidence, ready to conquer any adversary that dares to obstruct your path!

Imagine this scenario: you're preparing for a significant exam. Instead of cramming all your study into one sleep-deprived night (which would leave you resembling and feeling like a zombie), plan to divide your study sessions into manageable portions over several days and then adhere to your plan, even when you'd rather not. That, my dear friends, is the power of perseverance in all its glory! And the reward? Excelling in that exam, performing a victory jig, and feeling like you're on top of the world!

But what happens if you neglect to harness this remarkable power of perseverance? Well, picture standing before an intimidating wall and admitting defeat without even attempting to climb it. You'd miss out on the awe-inspiring view from the summit and the electrifying taste of triumph!

Our hero, Brainy Johnny, was a master at wielding the power of perseverance. He flexed his perseverance muscles daily, working **diligently**, maintaining unwavering focus, and never admitting defeat. And can you guess the result? He accomplished his goals speedier than a cheetah fuelled by sugar!

So, my brave friends, etch this into your minds: whenever you trip or tumble, hoist yourself up, brush off the dirt, stand tall, and forge ahead because, with perseverance, every challenge is merely another thrilling adventure awaiting your conquest!

And so, they all lived blissfully ever after, especially our Brainy Johnny, who continued to learn, evolve, and persevere, demonstrating that with the power of perseverance, no dream is too grand to realise.

The End.

Tongue Twister of this Story:

'Diligently' – This fancy word means doing something carefully and giving it your full attention. Think about when you're playing a game and really want to win, so you focus and try your best – that's being diligent! Or when you're doing your homework, and you make sure every answer is correct before you finish, you're working diligently. It's like being a superhero of hard work and focus!

On: Positive Affirmations

Once upon a time, a spirited little girl named Maria lived in the heart of a town nestled amidst gentle hills and whispering streams. Maria was a whirlwind of vivacity, her mind an endless wellspring of curiosity that thirsted for knowledge. Yet, when faced with a vexing maths problem or a tricky spelling challenge, she would be overcome by frustration, manifesting as tiny **tempests** of negativity.

Watching this recurring cycle, Maria's wise and loving mother, who could spot her daughter's frustration faster than a hawk spies its prey, decided to intervene. She introduced Maria to the captivating realm of positive affirmations – potent words brimming with transformative power, capable of bolstering her confidence and making her feel as invincible as her favourite comic book hero!

Maria's mum likened positive affirmations to sprinkling magical fairy dust over oneself. These empowering words, such as 'I am an unstoppable force' or 'I can conquer any challenge', acted like invisible cloaks that enveloped you in self-assurance and determination, endowing you with superpowers akin to those of legendary superheroes.

Each morning, as dawn painted the town in hues of gold and awakened the slumbering rooftops, Maria and her mum would rise together and recite five mighty affirmations:

1. "I can accomplish anything if I work hard for it."
2. "Whatever my mind can think and believe, I can achieve."
3. "Regardless of the magnitude of my fears, I possess the courage and wisdom to confront them."
4. "Today will be an extraordinary day!"
5. "I possess all the tools I need to triumph."

In no time, Maria began noticing a mesmerising transformation. Each time she murmured these affirmations, she felt her worries evaporate like dewdrops in the morning sun, and her confidence blossomed like a rose greeting the dawn. When a daunting exam loomed ahead or a perplexing assignment threatened to eclipse her joy, she would summon her affirmations as invisible shields, warding off the darts of doubt and fear.

To her astonishment, Maria found herself soaring above the clouds of uncertainty! Her teachers took note of her newfound confidence, and her grades began to glitter as brilliantly as her radiant smile. Even her classmates perceived the change, inspiring them to embrace the magical affirmations themselves.

Maria was profoundly thankful for the transformative power of these positive affirmations. They acted like a secret key, unlocking the treasure trove of her self-assurance and turning every obstacle into an exhilarating quest. Without these magical phrases, Maria wouldn't have unearthed the bravery to conquer her fears and reach for the moon. They helped her reveal the superpowers hidden within her, enabling her to accomplish extraordinary feats!

And so, Maria journeyed on, armed with her potent affirmations. She was prepared to take on the world, one thrilling adventure at a time.

The End.

Tongue Twister of this Story:

'Tempests' – This is another word for really big, wild storms. Imagine the wind blowing so hard it could almost push you over and rain pouring down like buckets of water from the sky; that's a tempest! It's like the biggest, loudest, wettest storm you could imagine!

On: Positive Energy

Once upon a time, a little girl named Mia lived in a world that mirrored ours. Ten years of age, with a smile as radiant as the midday sun, she had the rare ability to turn even the grouchiest **curmudgeon's** frown upside down. But Mia was not just any ordinary lass; she was a beacon of positive energy, a superheroine who scattered happiness like stardust wherever she ventured.

Mia steadfastly believed in the transformative potency of kindness and love. She grasped that positivity could morph any dreary situation into a vibrant spectacle, as colourful and joyful as a rainbow after a summer rain. Being in Mia's company was akin to diving into a bowl brimming with your favourite ice cream – a burst of delightful flavours, an express ticket to the land of gaiety!

One sunny afternoon, while the gentle breezes were teasing her hair into playful twirls, Mia was jauntily hopping her way home from school. Suddenly, she spotted a young lad sitting forlornly on the pavement. His face bore a sadness deeper than a panda deprived of its cherished bamboo shoots. Instantly, Mia knew she needed to drench this sad scene with her radiant positivity.

With a smile warmer than the first rays of dawn, Mia approached the boy, asking, "Is there anything I can do to brighten up your day?" What followed was a heartfelt exchange filled with laughter, shared anecdotes, and the sprouting of a fresh friendship.

The boy's spirits lifted, all thanks to the infectious positivity Mia radiated.

Mia stumbled upon a ground-breaking revelation on that memorable day: positive energy isn't merely magical; it's as contagious as a yawn during a monotonous lesson! A kind word or a warm smile can create ripples of joy that reach far and wide beyond one's wildest dreams. It's like an exhilarating game of tag, where everyone is 'it', and everyone emerges victorious!

Mia also discovered that being a beacon of positive energy uplifted those around her and filled her heart with a profound sense of contentment and joy, akin to finding the last missing piece of a jigsaw puzzle. From that day forward, Mia made a solemn pledge to herself. She vowed to keep her positivity ever-glowing, casting a warm light of good vibes wherever she roamed.

And so, our little ray of sunshine, Mia, continued her journey, inspiring everyone with her infectious positivity. She became a living testament to a priceless lesson: never underestimate the power of positive energy. This secret ingredient can transform any ordinary day into a remarkable adventure.

The End.

Tongue Twister of this Story:

'Curmudgeon' – This is a word we use to describe someone who is often grumpy, a bit like how you might feel when you have to do your chores before playing with your toys. This person usually likes to complain about things and doesn't smile much. Do you know how Mr Scrooge behaves in the stories? That's a good example of a curmudgeon!

On: Positive Language

Once upon a time, tucked away in a quaint little village, lived a bright-eyed lad named Jimmy. Jimmy was no run-of-the-mill boy; he was as one-of-a-kind as a snowflake, with a personality that sparkled just as much. His parents, Mr and Mrs Smith, were the embodiment of kindness, always treating everyone around them with respect and courtesy. They had a golden rule they lived by: 'always use good manners and polite words'. This rule was as precious to them as a well-kept family heirloom. Strangely enough, Jimmy seemed to struggle with this rule, forgetting it as easily as one loses a needle in a haystack.

When life decided to give Jimmy a tough time or when situations got as tangled as a bowl of spaghetti, Jimmy's instinct was to let out words as dark as a looming thunderstorm. However, one day, his parents decided they had had enough of Jimmy's tempestuous language.

They sat him down on their cosy, worn-out couch, its cushions as fluffy as clouds. They began to weave a story from their own youth, a time when they, too, had allowed bitter words to take control. With sincere words and lively gestures, they showed Jimmy how these harsh words could sting like nettles, hurting others and himself. Those stings felt even more painful when life was already serving him a platter of challenges!

After this enlightening story, they presented Jimmy with a challenge: to find a new, positive way to express his feelings. They explained that speaking with the warmth of a summer's day, instead of the iciness of a winter's night, benefits everyone – including himself. They told him that a person who uses positive language attracts good things like a magnet, such as friendships as delightful as ice cream on a hot day, opportunities as wide as the ocean, and a sense of well-being as comforting as a thick duvet on a frosty night.

With a spark of resolve in his eyes, Jimmy started paying attention to the words he used. He began replacing his gloomy phrases with ones that felt like a pat on the back. This new language, filled with positivity, gave him an extra spoonful of courage and a large helping of confidence to face whatever life tossed his way.

Instead of complaining, "This homework is tougher than wrestling a gorilla," he would say, "I'll break it down into manageable chunks until it becomes easy." Instead of moaning, "This looks like a **catastrophe** in the making!" he would reassure himself with, "I'll find the best solution, no worries."

Soon, Jimmy was experiencing the incredible power of positive words. Although initially challenging, like learning to swim without floaties, these uplifting phrases kept his spirits flying higher than a bird. His positive language spread joy like a field of blossoming daisies, brightening the day of everyone he met.

And so, we reach the end of our story about Jimmy, the boy who unlocked the superpower of positive words. Remember, dear friends; your words can be a storm cloud or a rainbow – the choice is entirely yours! Choose wisely, for the pen, or in this case, the tongue, is indeed mightier than the sword!

The End.

Tongue Twister of this Story:

'Catastrophe' – This is a word used to describe something really bad that happens. Imagine if you built a huge tower out of your favourite building blocks, and suddenly, it all falls down. That could feel like a catastrophe. It's a big word for a big problem or disaster.

On: Positive Thinking

Once upon a time, a bright-eyed young boy named Colin lived in a small, charming town named Dunnottar. At the tender age of ten, life seemed like a labyrinth to him, filled with puzzling turns, challenges to overcome, and a fair share of mundane tasks. The townsfolk often said, "Colin, you must learn to put on the spectacles of positivity!" But, alas, he was clueless about where to find these magical glasses that could transform his perspective of life.

One day, wandering in the enchanted forest brimming with whispering trees and magical beings, Colin stumbled over a hidden root. With a thud and a tumble, he found himself face-to-face with a radiant, fluttering fairy. She was hovering just above the ground, shimmering in every colour of the spectrum and even some hues that Colin had never laid eyes on! Intrigued and nursing his bruised pride, Colin plucked up his courage and queried her about this enigmatic concept everyone spoke of – 'positive thinking'.

With a sparkle in her eye that reflected the starlit sky above, she began to weave a story. "Positive thinking, dear child, is our secret armour! It's akin to a magic wand snugly placed in our pockets. This enchantment can help us surmount any mountain, no matter how tall, cross any river, no matter how wide, or decode any enigma, no matter how complex. It's all about backing yourself, concentrating on the 'I cans' rather than the 'I can'ts', and possessing the ability to spot a rainbow even amidst a downpour."

She continued, "When you allow positivity to **permeate** your being, your heart brims with joy as if you're on an endless carousel ride, stress evaporates, and your mind sharpens like a hawk's vision pinpointing its prey from afar, problems shrink to the size of marbles, friendships flourish like daffodils in spring, and your body feels as robust and unconquerable as a superhero!"

Colin's eyes glistened with awe as if trying to absorb every word she spoke. "Wow! How can I master this magic?" he eagerly asked. The sagacious fairy gave him a comforting smile that felt warm as a summer afternoon and shared her wisdom. She advised him to proclaim affirmations like, 'I'm a conqueror!' or, 'success is mine!' every dawn; to reflect on his blessings before he drifted off to sleep; to seek the silver lining in every dark cloud forever; and to remember that each stumble, each fall, is merely a new dance move waiting to be unveiled!

Back in school, Colin began applying this newfound enchantment. His grades rocketed skyward because he believed he could scale any academic peak. His laughter became infectious, magnetising many friends who wished to bask in his sunny character. Even his teachers admired his optimism and resolve, fostering a bond of trust that transformed classrooms into thrilling learning expeditions.

Colin often recalled that magical meetings in the forest throughout his life's voyage. The wise fairy's words had ignited a spark within him, turning him into a beacon of positivity that illuminated every room he entered. From then on, he felt that nothing was impossible. He knew that with his spectacles of positivity, he could gaze beyond the stars, past the moon, and into a cosmos teeming with boundless possibilities!

And so, Colin, the young adventurer, continued his journey, radiating positivity wherever he ventured, leading a life that was not just happily ever after but positively happily ever after.

The End.

Tongue Twister of this Story:

'Permeate' – This means to spread or soak through something completely. Imagine dropping a bit of food colouring into a glass of water. You'll see the colour spread out; eventually, it fills the whole glass. That's what 'permeate' means – just like how the colour fills the water, anything that permeates spreads or soaks through something else.

On: Procrastinating

Once upon a time, a lively little girl named Lucy lived in the whimsical land of Tick-Tock. With her rosy cheeks, twinkling eyes, and boundless energy, Lucy was always ready to embark on a thrilling adventure. Whether racing towards the swings as though competing in the Olympics or embarking on an exhilarating treasure hunt with her loyal companions, where 'X' marked the spot of hidden treasures, Lucy was always up for the challenge!

However, when it came to tasks that lacked the shimmer of excitement, like tidying up her room – which, to be frank, resembled a toy kingdom hit by a storm – or wrestling with the towering mountain of maths homework in her schoolbag, she would always say, "I'll do it in a jiffy." But, oh dear, that 'jiffy' seemed to stretch on forever, much like a rubber band that refused to recoil! The sticky web of procrastination had ensnared our spirited Lucy.

Now, you might wonder, what is this tongue-twister term called procrastination? Well, imagine your mum asking you to set the table for dinner while you're engrossed in watching your favourite online game. You respond, "I'll do it in a jiffy, Mum". But that 'jiffy' and many following 'jiffies' pass without action. That, my young friends, is procrastination! It could creep in while tackling any task, big or small, from organising your pencil case to mastering that tricky spelling challenge. Procrastination usually prowls around when the task feels as daunting as scaling Mount Everest or as dull as watching paint dry.

This habit of postponing our 'action hero moment' can lead to some sticky situations. Picture your mum being irked because she now has to set the dinner table herself while the scrumptious feast she prepared for you grows cold. Or missing out on splendid opportunities because you were too engrossed in trivial distractions. And guess what? That's precisely the predicament Lucy found herself in.

One day, an **epiphany** dawned upon Lucy. She realised that procrastination was about as useful as a chocolate teapot. She decided it was high time to change her strategy. Instead of putting off tasks, Lucy created mini-missions throughout her day. Her quests included conquering a chapter of her book before lunch or restoring order to her chaotic room by dinnertime.

These specific missions transformed her into a real-life superhero, much like a time-management wonder-girl. Lucy soon found her rhythm, and everything started to fall into place, just like a perfectly assembled jigsaw puzzle. And oh, the wonders she discovered! Her grades skyrocketed as she no longer risked forgetting a task or submitting it past the deadline. The cherry on top? Lucy bid farewell to stress because she was now on top of everything, with all tasks up-to-date and shipshape.

So, my fellow adventurers, here's a golden nugget of wisdom from Lucy's story. Don't delay when you've got something significant to tackle. Set yourself some achievable quests and keep ploughing ahead. That way, you can seize the splendid prizes life has in store!

And so, they lived happily ever after, promptly ticking off tasks and adventures every single day.

The End.

Tongue Twister of this Story:

'Epiphany' – This is like a light bulb moment. It's when you suddenly understand something that you didn't get before. It's like figuring out the answer to a tricky puzzle that has been confusing you for a while. Imagine you're trying to solve a tough maths problem, and then, suddenly, you get it – that's an epiphany!

On: Reflection

Once upon a time, a spirited young lad named Timmy lived in a bustling town. Timmy was no run-of-the-mill boy; he was a thrill-seeker, an adventurer, forever on a mission for new escapades and fresh ways to level up in the video game of life that every ten-year-old finds himself playing.

On one bright and sunny morning, his teacher entered the classroom, her eyes sparkling like distant galaxies. This wasn't any ordinary teacher; this was Miss Winkle, the most **sagacious** of educators with a heart brimming with wisdom and a suitcase filled with mesmerising stories. In her gentle voice, she introduced Timmy to a magical concept that was as captivating as it was enigmatic – reflection.

"Reflection?" Timmy blinked, his eyebrows furrowing in bewilderment. "You mean like what I see in the mirror?"

Miss Winkle laughed softly. "Not quite, my dear lad," she replied. "Reflection is like hopping aboard a time machine that whisks you back through your day. It's about plunging deep into the sea of your thoughts, replaying the day's events like scenes from a film, and comprehending how they've painted the tapestry of your day."

Timmy was intrigued. He fancied himself a detective, combing through the evidence of his day, connecting the dots, and piecing together the jigsaw puzzle that was his life. Miss Winkle proposed a daily ritual: a ten-minute pause at the end of each day committed to reflecting on his experiences, journaling the highs that made him fly and the lows that made him stumble, the victories that made him cheer, and the tumbles that made him tougher.

Timmy initially found this task as tricky as solving a Rubik's Cube whilst blindfolding and riding a unicycle! But our headstrong boy couldn't resist a challenge, so he rolled up his sleeves, donned his thinking cap, and persevered. Much like a caterpillar gradually metamorphosing into a butterfly, Timmy slowly began to untangle the threads of his day, spotting patterns like hidden star constellations, gaining invaluable lessons, and, most importantly, unravelling the marvellous mystery that was himself.

On days when Timmy felt the storm clouds looming overhead, he realised that he held the power to change the weather himself. He could flip the script, view the situation through a new lens, and find hidden silver linings in the darkest of clouds. With the aid of reflection, he discovered secret passages leading to solutions that had seemed as distant as the moon.

Before he knew it, reflection had woven itself into the fabric of his daily routine, becoming as essential as brushing his teeth, tying his shoelaces, or saving the last morsel of his favourite pudding for breakfast! No matter how the day unfolded – whether it was sunny or stormy, tranquil or tumultuous – he would consistently set aside some time to rewind, replay, and reflect.

Timmy was amazed by how this simple act of reflection transformed his life. It was as if he'd been handed a superhero cape, equipped with the power of insight and ready to conquer any dragon that dared to cross his path. Miss Winkle watched him with eyes shining brighter than the North Star, beaming with pride at how her little nugget of wisdom had turned into a goldmine for Timmy.

And so, our story draws to a close, but remember, just like Timmy, you also hold your own magic wand of reflection. Why not give it a twirl? Who knows what treasures you might unearth, what dragons you might defeat, what mountains you might scale!

The End.

Tongue Twister of this Story:

'Sagacious' – This is a big word, isn't it? Imagine you have a friend who is really good at figuring things out, like solving tough puzzles or knowing the best time to cross the road safely. They always seem to make smart decisions. That's what 'sagacious' means – being very wise or clever.

On: Reputation

Once upon a time, a delightful young girl named Lily lived in the quaint little town of Brakpan. With eyes that twinkled like the brightest star in the midnight sky and a spirit as vibrant as a hummingbird's wings, Lily was far from your average ten-year-old. She had an extraordinary wisdom that set her apart from her peers, much like a sunflower standing tall amongst a sea of daisies. Lily understood that a good reputation was not just valuable; it was a golden ticket to the grandest adventures in life's magnificent carnival.

Lily's parents, wise as the ancient oak trees and as cunning as the craftiest of foxes, had taught Lily from a tender age that a good reputation was akin to a magical key. This key, gleaming with infinite opportunities, could unlock trust as firm as a towering mountain, respect as deep as the vast ocean, and even a superhero-like credibility that would make even the strongest superheroes turn green with envy.

In the bustling hallways of her school, Lily was something of a mini-celebrity. Her reputation shone brighter than the disco ball at the annual school dance. Friends were drawn to her like bees to the most fragrant blossom, and when she spoke up in class, everyone listened as if she were weaving the most captivating fairy story. Teachers and classmates alike were always willing to lend her a helping hand, knowing well that Lily was as trustworthy as a promise carved into the heart of a diamond.

But you might wonder, how does one build such an admirable reputation? Well, my dear young friends, it's simpler than learning to tie the trickiest shoelaces! It involves **embodying** kindness that's as warm as a grandmother's embrace, doing the right thing even when no one's watching (much like a secret superhero on a covert mission), showing respect to the grown-ups in your world, and making decisions based on solid facts rather than fleeting feelings or gossip. Each of these actions is like a brick, and with patience and persistence, they build up to form a sturdy castle of good reputation.

However, it's crucial to understand that negative behaviours like lying or cheating act like a relentless storm, gradually eroding the foundations of your reputation castle. What took years to construct can crumble in mere seconds. Being rude or mean, especially without reason, is a sure-fire way to become as popular as a wasabi-flavoured ice cream sundae (yuck!).

As our story reaches its grand finale, Lily discovers that her gleaming reputation didn't just make her school days a breeze; it turned her into the remarkable, awe-inspiring person she was blossoming into. She realised that this golden ticket of a reputation would accompany her throughout her life's journey, helping her secure her dream job, find friends who mirrored her beautiful soul, and so much more.

Therefore, Lily understood that having a good name wasn't merely a part of living a good life; it was the secret ingredient in the world's most scrumptious chocolate cake. And let's be honest, who could resist a slice of that?

And so, we bid farewell to our story, but remember, the magic of a good reputation lives on.

The End.

Tongue Twister of this Story:

'Embodying' – This is a bit like when you act out a character from your favourite book or movie. You're not just pretending to be that character; you're trying to think, feel and behave exactly like them. It's as if you've become that character. That's what 'embodying' means – you're making something, like an idea or quality, a part of who you are.

On: Respect

Once upon a time, in the heart of a bustling town, two inseparable chums, Johnny and Jane, were having a whale of a time in the local park. Their infectious laughter echoed through the leafy trees, filling the air with joy as they played to their hearts' content. But then, they spotted a group of people who seemed as if they had zoomed down from the Planet of Dreadful Etiquette!

Johnny's eyes widened in astonishment, and he turned to Jane, exclaiming, "Blimey! That's not very jolly. Everyone should show respect wherever they roam."

"Respect?" Jane queried, her voice echoing curiosity. "What's that all about?"

Johnny scratched his head thoughtfully, pondering over the right words. Then, like a light bulb lighting up in a dark room, he enthusiastically answered, "Well, respect is like treating others how you'd want to be treated. It's about lending an ear when somebody speaks and responding with the magic words like 'please', 'thank you', and 'sorry'."

One glorious day, bathed in sunshine, Johnny demonstrated what respect looked like in action. He surrendered his seat on the spaceship (well, all right, it was a bus) to a tired-looking elderly person. He didn't receive a gleaming medal for his act, but the way his heart brimmed with pride made him feel every bit the superhero.

Jane also exhibited respect in her own unique manner. She used words as gentle as butterfly wings with her younger siblings, even when they were driving her around the bend. She understood that sprinkling kindness, even on challenging days, was the secret ingredient for building unbreakable bonds.

In the comfort of their home, they donned their thinking hats and concocted more ways to **disseminate** respect. They resolved that acknowledging everyone's unique traits and peculiarities would be their method of demonstrating respect. Whether it was different skin colours, beliefs, or viewpoints, they knew everyone should have the freedom to be their fabulous, eccentric selves without fear of being judged.

They understood that every act of respect, no matter how small it appeared, contributed to creating a big, beautiful world. They recollected a quote from school by the wise poet, Kahlil Gibran: 'Treat everyone with politeness, even those who are rude to you – not because they are nice, but because you are'.

Johnny and Jane believed that if everyone shared a slice of respect, the world would transform into a giant peace pizza (with extra cheese, of course!). Respect is all about celebrating diversity and giving everyone an equal chance to sparkle, no matter what.

And so they carried on their adventure, leaving a trail of respect in their wake, much like a rainbow following a summer shower. Their story serves as a gentle nudge that respect is the magic spice that can truly metamorphose the world.

The End.

Tongue Twister of this Story:

"Disseminate' – This is a word that means spreading something far and wide. Imagine making a cool drawing and wanting all your friends to see it. You'd be disseminating your drawing if you showed it to everyone in your school or even sent copies to other schools!

On: Responsibility

Once upon a time, a lively and adventurous boy named Arthur lived in the charming, cosy hamlet of Nigel. Arthur was quite the character, always wearing a cheeky grin, and his eyes sparkled with an unquenchable thirst for adventure. Yet, like many lads his age, Arthur had a certain knack for finding himself in a pickle, often neglecting the kind warnings of his doting parents, Mr and Mrs Clayton.

One bright and sunny afternoon, Arthur's penchant for mischief led him into a rather sticky wicket. On one of his daring escapades, he had taken his father's treasured pocket watch, a cherished family **heirloom**, and accidentally dropped it into the village well. A wave of fear washed over Arthur as he realised the enormity of his blunder. He could have easily spun a story or fibbed to avoid the repercussions, but something deep within him stirred.

He imagined the look of disappointment on his beloved father's face, and he decided to shoulder responsibility for his actions. With a heavy heart, he trudged back home, prepared to confess his error. His voice trembled as he stood before his mum and dad, but his eyes showed a steadfast resolve. He admitted his folly, and his parents were taken aback, not by the lost heirloom, but by their son's display of maturity.

Instead of criticising him, his parents commended Arthur. They expressed their pride, not for his mistake, but for his bravery in owning up to it. They explained that everyone sometimes stumbles and fumbles, but it takes courage to accept one's mistakes and face the consequences. Arthur felt an odd sense of relief wash over him. That day, he grasped that responsibility wasn't just about completing chores but also about being answerable for one's deeds.

From that day onwards, Arthur's perspective on life underwent a transformation. He carried on with his merry adventures, but he also started comprehending the significance of responsibility. Whenever he found himself in a tight spot, he remembered that pivotal day and chose to confront the truth, no matter how challenging it was. This newfound maturity earned him admiration not only from his family but also from his friends and teachers.

Through his journey, Arthur discovered that responsibility is a stepping stone towards wisdom and personal growth. His story reminds us that it's all right to trip and fall, as long as we're ready to learn from our mistakes and accept them. After all, it's through our blunders that we grow and evolve into better versions of ourselves.

And so, Arthur's story concludes, but the lessons he learned continue to inspire. Remember, taking responsibility is not just about dealing with consequences; it's about maturing and learning to better oneself. And that, dear friends, is the true magic of responsibility.

The End.

Tongue Twister of this Story:

'Heirloom' – This is a special item that has been in your family for a very long time, usually passed down from one generation to the next. It could be something like your great-grandma's favourite necklace or your grandad's old watch. These items are not just valuable because they might be made of expensive materials, but they're also precious because they carry lots of family memories and history with them.

On: Rest and Sleep

Once upon a moonlit night, in a town that might look and feel just like yours or mine, lived an extraordinary young lad named Jack. Jack was no ordinary boy; he was a prodigy, a living dictionary, always brimming with curiosity and eager to absorb every bit of knowledge that came his way. He had dreams as vast as the sky and ambitions that towered higher than the tallest mountain. But, every superhero has an **Achilles heel**, and Jack's was his struggle to keep his eyes open and his mind sharp during school hours.

Now, don't misunderstand; Jack was not lazy or uninterested. Quite the contrary! He was a nocturnal creature, a night owl. The moon was his daylight, and the stars, his companions. While the world lay silent and asleep, Jack would be alert and active, reading, contemplating, and journeying through the realms of knowledge. But when morning dawned, Jack was in a fierce battle with his most formidable adversary: the cruel, relentless alarm clock. Regardless of how many times he hit snooze, it would ring persistently, constantly reminding him of his sleep deprivation.

Every day, Jack would trudge into school, his eyes weighed down with fatigue and his yawns echoing louder than a lion's roar. He would brush it off, thinking it was trivial, not understanding that his lack of sleep was slowly turning his turbocharged brain into a sluggish snail.

On a sun-kissed day, his observant teacher, blessed with an eagle's sharp eyes and an owl's wisdom, noticed Jack's drooping eyelids and wavering concentration. "My dear boy," she asked him gently, "are you getting enough sleep every night?" Jack pondered this question, his mind wandering back to the countless nights he had spent studying under the dim light of his desk lamp.

Wanting to guide him, his teacher disclosed the secret of the enchanting realm of sleep. "When you welcome the sandman into your life, your body stores energy, just like a super-powered battery, ready to fuel you for the next day," she explained, creating an image of a world where sleep was the superhero everyone needed.

Suddenly, everything fell into place in Jack's mind. He understood that he needed to befriend the sandman if he wanted to excel in school, achieve his dreams, and be the prodigy he knew he could be. He needed to aim for at least eight hours of restful sleep every night. This was the secret sauce to keeping his mind sharp, his thoughts focused, and his energy levels soaring.

Determined, Jack set out on a mission to establish new, sleep-friendly habits. He said goodbye to his gadgets an hour before bedtime, choosing instead to immerse himself in the enchanting world of storybooks. He swapped his late-night explorations with a calming bath or shower and started jotting down his thoughts or worries so they wouldn't disturb his peaceful slumber.

The transformation was astounding. Jack was rejuvenated. He became more energetic and lively during the day. His brain worked like a well-oiled machine on tests and projects. He was pleasantly surprised but, more importantly, he felt a sense of accomplishment. Over time, Jack discovered the incredible benefits of a good night's sleep. It made him stronger, smarter, and happier. It reduced his stress levels and honed his focus. He recognised that sleep wasn't merely important; it was super-duper important!

The cherry on top? Bedtime didn't have to be dull. With some cool habits like setting boundaries between work and play, creating a cosy sleep sanctuary, munching on nutritious snacks, and incorporating regular exercise, anyone could stay alert and active all day.

And that's how Jack, the knowledge-thirsty prodigy, transformed into Jack, the well-rested whizz-kid. And he lived happily (and well-rested) ever after, inspiring others to embrace the magic of sleep.

Remember, sleep is your secret superpower, too. Use it wisely and, like Jack, you can conquer all your dreams!

The End.

Tongue Twister of this Story:

'Achilles heel' – Imagine you're really good at playing football, but there's one thing you struggle with, like kicking the ball with your left foot. That weakness is your 'Achilles heel'. The name comes from a story about a Greek hero named Achilles who was very strong and brave but had one weak spot – his heel.

On: Sadness

Once upon a time, a delightful little girl named Sarah lived in the pulsing core of a vibrant metropolis. Sarah was no ordinary child. She danced through life with a spring in her step, found enchantment in everyday things, and viewed the world not merely as it was but brimming with endless possibilities. Sarah was like a radiant sunbeam, her spirit as bright and warm as the golden sun on a perfect summer's day. And her smile, ah, her smile! It was like a beacon in the darkest storm, guiding lost sailors back to the safety of the shore.

However, life, being the unpredictable journey that it is, had a twist in store for our young heroine. A dark cloud rolled over Sarah's technicolour world on an otherwise ordinary day, casting eerie shadows everywhere. A sting of sadness, a feeling Sarah had only briefly encountered before, began to dominate her life. This wasn't just the disappointment of losing her favourite stuffed toy or the frustration of misplacing her beloved comic book. A profound emptiness made her feel like a tiny boat adrift in a vast, directionless ocean.

Her once cherished activities now seemed devoid of colour, as if a rainbow had been stripped of all its vibrant hues. Even the most delicious ice cream tasted no better than plain old vanilla. Sarah began to distance herself from her friends and family, retreating into her shell like a frightened turtle, feeling as if she were alone on a deserted island.

Watching their usually **exuberant** daughter transform, Sarah's parents, who were as wise and brave as superheroes, decided to have a meaningful chat with her. This conversation would be as impactful as any superhero mission.

"Sarah," they began gently, "life is like a rollercoaster. There are times when you're flying high, touching the sky, and then there are moments when you're plunging down at a dizzying speed. And that's perfectly normal."

They explained that sadness was as much a part of life as happiness. It wasn't a terrifying monster lurking under the bed but a friend who visited occasionally, teaching us valuable lessons about ourselves. They encouraged her to express her feelings, find joy even in the simplest things, be patient with herself, and, most importantly, understand that it's perfectly okay not to be okay sometimes.

They also introduced Sarah to depression, describing it as an intense kind of sadness that overstays its welcome. If sadness could be likened to a rainy day, then depression was like a relentless monsoon. But just like any monsoon, it could be weathered with the right help and support.

Armed with this newfound wisdom, Sarah began to navigate her sea of emotions with newfound confidence. She still had days when the grey cloud cast its shadow, but now she knew it wasn't a permanent guest in her life. She realised she was not alone on her island; she had a tribe of people who loved her dearly and were ready to brave any storm by her side.

And, most importantly, Sarah discovered that after every storm, there's a rainbow waiting to be found. And after the darkest night, there's always a dawn.

From that point, our little heroine continued her journey, facing the downs with courage, savouring the ups, and growing stronger with each passing day. Sarah's story is a tribute to the resilience of the human spirit and a gentle reminder that even in the face of adversity, we can rise again.

So here's to Sarah, the young girl who taught us that it's okay to feel sad, that talking about our feelings is crucial, and that no matter how fierce the storm may be, there's always a rainbow waiting on the other side.

The End.

Tongue Twister of this Story:

'Exuberant' – This is a big word that means you're full of energy, excitement, and happiness. It's like when you feel so joyful and lively that you can't help but jump around or laugh out loud. Imagine how you feel on your birthday morning when you're super excited about the presents and the party – that's being exuberant!

On: Self-Belief

Once upon a time, a bright-eyed, zest-filled girl named Simona lived in a small village called Sea Point. This wasn't an ordinary village, and Simona was far from an ordinary girl. She had the determination of a honey bee building its hive and dreams as plentiful as the stars that dot the night sky. Yet, she was as shy as a bunny hiding in a burrow, which meant she had few friends with whom to share her grand aspirations.

The villagers were a contrasting lot. They didn't carry dreams in their hearts but rather words that shattered dreams, like 'impossible', 'not advisable', and 'unachievable'. They constantly told Simona her dreams were as unlikely as elephants learning to pirouette. But our brave Simona, chin up and eyes gleaming with resolve, decided to turn their scepticism into her motivation. She used their **pessimism** as a catapult to launch herself towards her dreams.

Every day, Simona worked harder than a squad of ants preparing for winter. She devoted every ounce of her energy and passion to her dreams. Before long, people started noticing more than her reserved demeanour. At the grand village fair, they saw a girl whose energy shone brighter than the most dazzling fireworks. Yet, some villagers scoffed and murmured behind cupped hands, declaring her efforts futile as a marshmallow hammer. They only saw the radiant exterior, not the sweat, tears, and unwavering determination that made it glow.

One grey Tuesday, as Simona was plodding home from school, her spirits as low as a sunken ship, she encountered an old man with hair as white as snow. Seeing Simona's crestfallen face, he asked why she looked as disheartened as a wilted sunflower. Simona then shared her story of disparaging whispers and her plummeting morale.

The old man listened, his eyes sparkling with the wisdom of ages. He said, "Simona, don't let the critics clip your wings. Trust in yourself because that's mightier than a lion's roar. You can become whatever you dream of, just like a seed grows into a towering tree."

Simona's eyes opened wide, and realisation dawned on her like the first light of day. Self-belief was the secret sauce to making her dreams rise like phoenixes from the ashes. The old man got up and said, "Always remember, Simona, your mind is a magical wand. If you can dream it and believe it, you can achieve it."

From that day forward, Simona donned those words like a knight's armour, her protection against the world. Whenever life decided to play a game of chess or made unpredictable moves, she would pause, recall the old man's counsel, and summon the bravery to make her next move. She knew that with self-belief, she could scale any cliff, no matter how steep, or cross any river, no matter how turbulent.

And so, Simona showed everyone that even the impossible becomes possible if you have faith in yourself. After all, who needs pirouetting elephants when you have a girl like Simona soaring on the wings of her dreams?

The End.

Tongue Twister of this Story:

'Pessimism' – This is when someone often thinks that bad things will happen. It's like when you always expect it to rain, even on a sunny day, or think your football team will lose before the match even starts. Pessimists often see the glass as half empty, not half full.

On: Selflessness

Once upon a time, nestled between the hustle and bustle of a colossal city and the serene whispers of the countryside, lay a little village. This wasn't just any ordinary village; it was a place where the inhabitants carried hearts as grand and radiant as the moon, their kindness illuminating even the darkest corners.

In this village of boundless compassion was a young lad named Jaden. Despite being only ten, his spirit of **benevolence** soared higher than the tallest skyscrapers, reflecting the very essence of the village he called home.

One sunny afternoon, while Jaden was deeply engrossed in an exciting race of paper boats in a puddle, a sight caught his sharp eyes. Mr Oldman, the wise elder of the village, seemed to be struggling with sacks of wheat. These sacks were so heavy they could give a hefty hippo a run for its money!

Without a moment's hesitation, Jaden rushed to Mr Oldman's side, his feet moving faster than a sprinting cheetah. Offering his assistance, he hoisted the burdensome sacks onto his small shoulders. His sparkling eyes and infectious smile melted the heaviness of the task at hand, making the journey homeward feel like a delightful walk through a candy-filled wonderland.

Jaden's selfless gesture deeply touched Mr Oldman. He showered blessings on the young boy and applauded his act of kindness. He declared that Jaden's actions were a powerful reminder that kindness knows no age.

Jaden's story is a glowing testament to the virtue of selflessness. It's about becoming a superhero, not by possessing superpowers, but by helping those in need. It's about being a ray of sunshine, brightening someone's day without expecting anything in return.

Being selfless is like being a sprinkler of joy, watering the world with happiness and watching it blossom – one act of kindness at a time. And the most magical part? When others witness your kindness, they might catch the 'kindness bug' too!

Practising selflessness can be as simple as holding the door for someone, helping an elderly person cross the street, or offering your last piece of candy to a friend. You could also volunteer at a local shelter or donate your old toys. Each act of kindness, no matter how small, is a step towards making the world a better place.

So, the golden nugget from our story is this: being selfless is akin to being a joy-spreading magician, while being selfish is like being a grumpy goblin hoarding his treasure. Spoiler alert – grumpy goblins aren't known for their happiness. Let's choose to be joyous magicians instead, sprinkling happiness wherever we go!

And so, with hearts brimming with joy and kindness, they all lived happily ever after.

The End.

Tongue Twister of this Story:

'Benevolence' – This is like being the kindest and nicest person you can be. It's when you do good things for others without expecting anything in return. Imagine giving your last sweet to a friend just because you want them to be happy – that's benevolence!

On: Self-Love

Once upon a time, in the charming and vibrant town of Aylesbury, a little girl with eyes that sparkled brighter than the most dazzling star lived. This little girl was named Page and held the heart-warming title of the 'Kindness Queen' among the townsfolk. Her reputation for sharing extended to everything she possessed.

From her delightful strawberry ice creams on warm summer days to her infectious laughter that could lighten up even the gloomiest room and her comforting bear hugs that felt like the warmest blanket on a cold winter night. But, there was a puzzle that Page couldn't quite solve – how could she express the same kindness to herself as she did so freely to others?

As the days gracefully waltzed into weeks, Page continued her mission of sprinkling kindness, like magical stardust, all around. Yet, the mystery of self-kindness remained unsolved. She wondered why her heart fluttered like a butterfly when she shared her joy with others but felt as heavy as a mountain when she tried to save some happiness for herself. Surely, spreading joy should fill her own heart with happiness too?

One sunny morning, an adventure beckoned Page! She and her family boarded a gleaming silver aeroplane for an exciting journey. As they soared above the clouds, a flight attendant's voice echoed through the cabin… "Remember, put on your own oxygen mask first before assisting others."

Page knitted her brows in confusion. *Why should I help myself before helping others?* she thought. With this question twirling in her mind, she gazed out at the endless sky. Then, the meaning of the message dawned on her. Just like securing her oxygen mask first, she needed to love herself first before being able to spread love and kindness to others. Only from a position of strength can you safely help others. The more joy she discovered within herself, the brighter she could shine for everyone around her.

From that moment of revelation onwards, Page embarked on a beautiful self-love journey. She started listening to the whispers of her heart, taking breaks from the fast-paced digital world to soak in the soothing symphony of nature, and making every night a snuggle-fest with her cosy bed. She began to savour foods that made her feel strong and energetic and started viewing her mistakes as stepping stones leading to the castle of success.

As the days transformed into weeks, Page's journey of self-love began to change her. She radiated warmth like she had swallowed a tiny sun. Her newfound self-love potion brewed a sparkling confidence within her, casting a magical **aura** around her. This magic boosted her school grades and sprinkled her friendships with the essence of strength and positivity.

Page arrived at a heart-warming realisation. If everyone added a pinch of self-love into their lives, the world would become a joy-filled playground. So, let's all learn from Page's story: self-love isn't just the cherry on top of the cake; it's the entire scrumptious cake! When we love ourselves, we can sweeten the world and create a happier place for all.

So, dear friends, this isn't the end of the story but rather the thrilling beginning of your own adventure of self-love! Let your journey begin now!

Remember, every step you take towards loving yourself is a step towards brightening the world with your unique light. So, shine on, dear friends, and let your journey of self-love transform you into the brightest star in the universe.

The End.

Tongue Twister of this Story:

'Aura' – An aura is like an invisible bubble surrounding each person. Think of it like the glow around a light bulb. It's a special kind of energy that can change colours based on how we feel. For example, our aura might be bright and colourful when we're happy. When we're sad or upset, it might turn darker. Not everyone can see auras, but some believe they can sense or feel them.

On: Setting Goals

Once upon a time, in a kingdom painted with the dazzling colours of dreams and infinite possibilities, there resided an extraordinary young girl named Ava. Ava was no ordinary child; her eyes sparkled brighter than the most splendid northern lights, and her dreams soared higher than the majestic Mount Everest and plunged deeper than the Mariana Trench. She harboured a dream that seemed larger than life itself – she envisioned herself as a bona fide astronaut, donning a gleaming space helmet and reaching for the stars!

However, dreams as colossal as Ava's often cast long, daunting shadows of doubt and fear. There were times when Ava felt like a tiny ant standing before a vast anthill, questioning how she could possibly overcome such a monumental task.

Ava's wise and loving parents aided her in one such moment of wavering uncertainty. Their warm smiles radiated reassurance, their words acting as a lighthouse guiding Ava through her stormy sea of doubts. "Ava," they said gently, "the secret to climbing any mountain, no matter how towering it may seem, lies in setting goals!"

Now, you might be wondering what these 'goals' are. Picture them as magical treasure maps, each line and curve guiding you towards your dreams. These maps can lead you to treasures both nearby and far away. A short-term goal might be mastering a challenging maths problem, while a long-term goal might be as grand and awe-inspiring as becoming an astronaut!

Setting goals is like having your personal cheerleading squad constantly propelling, encouraging, and applauding you to scale new heights. Every goal you achieve, every milestone you reach, is a triumphant win for Team You! It instils in you a sense of accomplishment and joy that screams, "Yes, I did it!" And who wouldn't want to revel in such glory?

Moreover, setting goals allows you to break down your enormous dream into smaller, more manageable pieces. It's like slicing a large, **delectable** pizza into bite-sized pieces that you can relish one at a time. This process helps you prioritise tasks, monitor progress, and make necessary adjustments if you veer off course.

For those passionate about sports or music, setting goals can be your secret weapon to hone your focus, accelerate your improvement, and taste the sweet nectar of victory even sooner!

The best part? Setting goals triggers a journey of self-discovery. It's like peering into a mirror reflecting your soul, unearthing your strengths, accepting your weaknesses, and shaping yourself into the best version you can be.

Once Ava understood this wisdom, she began to set her goals and chart her course towards the stars. She pursued them relentlessly, taking one small but significant step at a time, always dreaming big, always reaching for the stars.

So, what's the valuable lesson from Ava's magical story? Everyone should strive to set meaningful, achievable goals regardless of age or stature. The true enchantment lies in ensuring you accomplish them!

Armed with this newfound wisdom, they lived happily ever after – setting goals, achieving dreams, and leaving their unique mark on the tapestry of the universe.

And so the story ends, but remember, every ending is just a new beginning!

The End.

Tongue Twister of this Story:

'Delectable' – We use this word to describe something that's really, really yummy. It's like when you take a bite of your favourite chocolate cake, and it tastes so good that you can't help but say, "Mmm, this is delectable!" It's like saying something is so delicious you can't get enough of it.

On: Standards

Once upon a time, in a land bathed in eternal sunshine, nestled just where the sky kissed the earth, there lived a lively and curious boy named Tommy. Tommy was a riddle wrapped in a mystery, with his school assignments playing a sly game of hide-and-seek, household tasks dodging him like swift swallows in flight, and the golden rules of behaviour often slipping from his memory like sand through his fingers.

On a day that began no different from any other, under the persistent glow of the sun, Tommy's parents decided to share with him a secret formula. This formula wasn't for his most cherished, ooey-gooey, and delightfully crispy chocolate chip cookies, but, rather, it was a guide to sail through life's vast oceans. They sat him down, their eyes burrowing into his like miners seeking precious gems, and said, "Tommy, we want you to remember this always: the way you do one thing is the way you do everything!" They further explained that it wasn't about chasing perfection like a wild goose. Instead, it was about consistently giving his best effort, not just when fortune smiled upon him or when tasks were as easy as blowing bubbles.

Tommy replied with a puzzled frown, scratching his head in confusion, then fell into a profound silence. After a moment, a spark ignited! Like a lighthouse illuminating the darkest sea, he decided to embrace this new **mantra** wholeheartedly. Homework was no longer a bitter pill to swallow; it became an exciting treasure hunt for knowledge. Tommy started seeking help to master each challenge instead of hurriedly jotting down answers to finish the task. Even chore time turned into an exciting quest. Tommy ensured his tasks, even those he previously considered a bother – like taking out the trash – were done thoroughly without any shortcuts or hidden escape routes!

Whenever Tommy had to make decisions, whether big or small or when interacting with others, he became a pint-sized Socrates. He'd stop, consider the advantages and disadvantages, balance the good against the bad, and then make decisions fortified with his newfound wisdom that proudly upheld high standards.

Days turned into weeks, weeks transformed into months, and something magical happened. The people around Tommy began to notice a big change in him. He was no longer the forgetful, shortcut-taking, occasional rule-defying boy. He had bloomed into Mr Consistent, upholding high standards in every aspect of his life. The newfound respect from his friends and elders was the icing on the cake, but the true victory lay in how Tommy now saw himself. His heart brimmed with pride and self-assurance, all because he lived by his parents' golden mantra.

This story, my dear young friends, is a soft nudge reminding you that setting high goals, reaching for the stars, being consistent, and holding yourself to high standards can be your magic key to unlocking success and self-appreciation. Remember, the way you do one thing is the way you do everything!

And so, they continued to live happily, learning, growing, and evolving forever after.

The End.

Tongue Twister of this Story:

'Mantra' – A mantra is a bit like a special sentence or phrase people repeat to themselves. Imagine feeling a bit scared before a big football match, and you repeatedly tell yourself, *I can do this; I'm brave* – that's a bit like a mantra. It's used to help people feel better, more focused, or even calm.

On: Staying Healthy

Once upon a time, in the colourful town of Adventureville, there resided a dynamic and lively young lady named Sally. She was as vibrant as a fireworks display on Bonfire Night, brimming with zest and an infectious spirit. Her days were spent scampering around the town's lush parkland, engaging in spirited games of tag with her chums, leaving a trail of merriment and laughter wherever she went.

However, one day, as if a bright lantern had been switched on above her, Sally had a significant revelation. She understood that staying healthy was not merely about who could sprint the fastest or leap the highest. It was about the decisions she made every day to maintain her physical strength and keep her mind as sharp as a just-sharpened pencil.

Armed with this newfound understanding, Sally decided she wanted to be as robust as Wonder Woman and as agile as Batgirl to sustain her thrilling escapades. She discovered the secret to this superhero transformation involved eating fruits and vegetables of all rainbow colours, crunching on whole grains that gifted her with boundless energy, and sipping magic potions, otherwise known as water, to keep her well-hydrated.

Next, Sally unravelled another enchanting secret: the rejuvenating power of sleep. Just as her favourite toy robot required an overnight charge to operate, Sally's body, too, needed plenty of rest to refresh itself. And the best bit? Her dreams took her on extraordinary journeys where she rode on shimmering unicorns and conversed with talking animals!

But the marvels didn't stop there. Sally soon understood that exercise was more than just flexing muscles or setting new records. It was akin to the steady rhythm of her heart, a beautiful symphony that kept her healthy and cheerful and filled her life with sunshine. Exercise became an **indispensable** part of her daily routine, from thrilling bicycle races with her friends to spontaneous dance-offs in her bedroom to the beats of her favourite songs.

As Sally matured from a young sapling into a tall, sturdy oak tree, she acknowledged that the healthy habits she had been cultivating were akin to tiny seeds. Over time, they grew into towering trees that bore the fruits of wellness throughout her life. She had more concentration at school, was stronger on the football pitch, and was overflowing with positive energy. The seeds of good health she had sown in her childhood had sprouted into a lush forest of well-being in her adulthood.

Sally realised that being healthy was not just about appearing good on the outside; it was like possessing a superpower that illuminated her life from within, making it brighter, happier, and more fulfilling. With this newfound comprehension, she embarked on a lifelong mission to be the healthiest version of herself.

The journey wasn't always smooth. There were choppy waters to navigate and colossal monsters to conquer. But Sally's story serves as a treasure map for each one of us, reminding us that the most significant adventure we can embark on is the pursuit of health and happiness.

So, brave adventurers, always remember it's never too early to start your journey towards health. Equip yourself with the compass of knowledge, pack your rucksack with nutritious fruits and vegetables, and set sail on this thrilling voyage together!

The End.

Tongue Twister of this Story:

'Indispensable' – Imagine you have a favourite toy you always play with and can't think of having fun without it. 'Indispensable' is just a fancy word for something just like that – something or someone so important you can't do without. It's like your favourite toy is 'indispensable' to your playtime!

On: The Golden Rule

Once upon a time, a pleasant young boy named Jack lived in a land not so far away. He was known throughout the kingdom for his heart of gold, though he had a knack for stumbling over it in his attempts to bond with his companions. Jack, the class clown, was always armed with a joke or a jest, believing it all to be harmless fun. However, his friends often found themselves nursing hurt feelings rather than sharing in his laughter.

One particularly sunny afternoon, one of Jack's buddies stopped by, carrying a golden nugget of wisdom from the vast vaults of their school's knowledge bank. This wisdom was called the 'Golden Rule'. As glittery as a hidden pirate's treasure, the rule proclaimed: if you desire to be treated like royalty, you must extend the same courtesy to others. Jack was intrigued by this idea and eager to learn about incorporating this gleaming rule into his life.

His friend simplified it for him. If you act like a grumpy gremlin, others will likely reciprocate. But if you're as sweet as a candy-coated gummy bear, they'll probably shower you with sweetness in return! His friend further explained that this rule was universal. It applied to everyone – family, friends, the friendly ice cream vendor, and even the sour-faced neighbours down the street.

Everyone, after all, deserves a warm smile and a friendly high-five because it's the cool thing to do. With newfound **enlightenment**, Jack embraced the

Golden Rule as his guiding principle. He made it his mission to treat everyone with kindness and respect as if they were celebrities. While it wasn't always a walk in the park, whenever he faced a difficult situation, he would ask himself, *What would the Golden Rule do?*

This subtle shift in his approach transformed Jack into a bona fide superhero of kindness. Whether helping his friends tackle their terrifying math homework or simply scattering compliments as generously as a flower girl tossing petals at a wedding, Jack was on a mission! Soon enough, those around him felt more loved and valued than ever, thanks to Jack's kindness crusade.

The cherry on top? Jack's new golden philosophy helped him make a plethora of new friends. He also earned a shiny badge of respect that he wore with pride. He realised that, despite our differences or the sticky situations we might find ourselves in, everyone can strike gold by living by the Golden Rule: always treat others as you would like to be treated.

And so our young hero continued his journey, spreading kindness and joy wherever he went, demonstrating that the Golden Rule isn't just golden; it's downright spectacular. Jack had discovered a secret recipe for friendship and respect and was eager to share it with the world.

In the end, Jack didn't just live happily ever after; he lived kindly, generously, and joyfully ever after. And he ensured everyone else did, too, because that's the true magic of the Golden Rule.

The End.

Tongue Twister of this Story:

'Enlightenment' – You know when you're trying to solve a tough puzzle, and suddenly, you understand how all the pieces fit together? That moment of understanding is a bit like 'enlightenment'. It's a fancy word we use to describe the feeling when you learn something new that makes you see things differently and more clearly. Everything becomes easier to see and understand, like switching on a light in a dark room. That's 'enlightenment'!

On: The Law of Attraction

Once upon a time, a little visionary named Emma resided in a universe where the moon was as luminous and golden as a cheddar wheel. Her mind was a radiant, ever-twinkling kaleidoscope of ideas, ceaselessly humming with wonderment, buzzing like an **industrious** honeybee with questions about everything from the dew-kissed grass to the star-studded cosmos. Emma was a dreamer whose dreams were as colossal as the highest mountain of ice cream you could imagine, teeming with rainbow sprinkles and crowned with a cherry. But she wasn't merely a dreamer – she was also a doer, always eager to transform her dreams into reality.

She stumbled upon an intriguing concept on a day radiant with sunshine while surfing the boundless ocean of knowledge on her gleaming iPad. It was called 'the law of attraction', and it intrigued her as much as an ancient treasure map in an adventure story. Intrigued, Emma decided to delve into this newfound knowledge, much like a brave explorer embarking on an epic voyage.

To her surprise, the law of attraction was no less than a magical charm! It was akin to a super-powered magnet nestled in the labyrinth of your mind. If one filled their thoughts with joy and positivity, they'd attract more sunshine into their life. On the flip side, if one harboured gloomy thoughts, they might as well prepare for a downpour!

Emma's eyes sparkled with exhilaration. "This seems like a thrilling rollercoaster ride," she mused and donned her imaginary helmet, visualising her wishes as though they had already come true. These wishes included acing her maths test, discovering the perfect tree for her secret treehouse, and owning a pet unicorn (because, let's face it, who wouldn't want that?).

Each time something remarkable occurred, like receiving an A+ in art or discovering a spectacular shell on the beach, she'd give her reflection a sly wink and whisper, "Thanks, law of attraction!"

Emma soon understood that this magical law wasn't just for petty wishes. It was more like a golden key that could unlock even her most ambitious dreams – dreams such as being the youngest astronaut to step foot on Mars or establishing a world-renowned cookie business that would make everyone's taste buds do a happy dance. To attain these dreams, she had to be crystal-clear about what she wanted, break down her dream into manageable chunks akin to cookie bites, and then savour those bites one by one.

The most thrilling aspect was feeling like she was the author of her own enchanting story! But Emma also discovered a crucial lesson: if she allowed negative thoughts to occupy her mind, they'd invite their gloomy pals over, too. So, she made it her mission to keep her thoughts as vibrant and joyous as a rainbow following a refreshing summer shower.

So, my young adventurers, if you're eager to try this law of attraction, here's the secret formula. Firstly, understand precisely what you want, as clearly as you know your favourite ice cream flavour (mine is mint chocolate chip, just so you know).

Then, fragment your grand dream into mini objectives akin to levels in your preferred video game. Believe in yourself as passionately as you believe in magic. And finally, continue advancing towards your dream, taking one brave step at a time each day.

With perseverance, a hearty dose of determination, and a liberal sprinkle of positive thinking, you can make your wildest dreams come true! Remember, the journey to your goals might be winding and full of unexpected twists and turns, akin to a thrilling rollercoaster ride, but with bravery in your heart and tenacity in your spirit, you can accomplish anything you set your mind to. What you focus on is what you manifest!

And so, they all lived happily ever after...

The End.

Tongue Twister of this Story:

'Industrious' – You know how some people are always busy doing things, like homework or chores, and they hardly ever sit still because they're always finding something productive to do? That's what we call 'industrious'. It's like being a busy bee who's always making honey. So, if someone is 'industrious', they work hard and are really good at getting things done.

On: Trustworthiness

Once upon a time, in a whimsical kingdom known as Lollipop Land, where houses were constructed from candy canes and jelly beans sprouted from trees, lived an extraordinary ten-year-old boy named Billy Bobblehead. Billy was no ordinary boy; he was a living bobblehead, his head bouncing joyously like a basketball on a trampoline! But what made Billy truly extraordinary wasn't his bobbing head but rather the golden virtue that dwelled within his heart – his unwavering trustworthiness.

Billy's parents woke up every dawn with grins that outshone the morning sun. They were the parents of a truth-telling **prodigy**. Billy's honesty was so steadfast that even on days when telling the truth was as appealing as devouring broccoli without any cheese sauce, he could easily outsmart a lie detector test.

Billy's wise parents, as knowledgeable as ancient owls, had instilled in him from an early age that trustworthiness was the golden key to life's treasure chest. They taught him that honesty is like a boomerang; it always comes back to you, often carrying extra treats. Just imagine tossing a stick and getting back a colossal chocolate chip cookie in return! Sounds delicious, doesn't it?

Billy's trustworthiness turned him into a beacon of reliability in Lollipop Land. Billy was your boy if you needed someone to safeguard your secret candy stash. If you needed to share a secret about your secret crush, Billy's heart, secure as a vault, was ready to keep it. When Billy spoke, people listened with rapt attention, knowing he was as genuine as they come.

As Billy catapulted into his teenage years, his trustworthiness helped him stand tall and propelled him to new heights. It became his golden ticket, granting him access to incredible opportunities. He even landed the role of the official taste tester at the local ice cream parlour because everyone knew Billy was as dependable as a Swiss timepiece. Now, isn't that the dream job?

Nonetheless, life isn't always about rainbows and sparkles. A lack of trustworthiness can be as painful as stepping barefoot on an unnoticed Lego piece. If your words wobble like jelly, people might start seeing you as the town jester and stop taking you seriously. It's like donning a clown outfit to a black-tie event – completely inappropriate!

Trustworthiness is the ultimate power-up in the video game of life. It helps you level up, gaining respect from family, friends, and even the gruff neighbour who always seems to be under his personal rain cloud. It's like a gleaming badge that declares, 'Hey, I'm authentic! You can rely on me'.

The grandest reward? Billy always felt this warm, cosy sensation akin to wearing fluffy socks on a frosty winter day. He knew that by choosing truth over deceit, he wasn't just triumphing in the game of life but also setting unbeatable high scores!

So, dear friends, that's the enchanting story of Billy Bobblehead, the truth-telling hero from Lollipop Land. As we draw the curtains on our story with the sun setting in the background, let's strive to be like

Billy because honesty indeed is the best policy. And who knows, it might even earn you some free ice cream or perhaps a gigantic chocolate chip cookie!

The End.

Tongue Twister of this Story:

'Prodigy' – Okay, so you know how some kids are really, really good at something? Like they can play the piano beautifully even though they're still young, or they can solve super difficult maths problems that even some adults can't do? That's what we call a 'prodigy'. It's like being a superhero, but instead of flying or super strength, their special power is being amazing at something like music, maths, or sports.

On: Visualisation

Once upon a time, in a universe where the stars twinkled like the peals of giggles from children at play, there resided a star sprinter – a young lass named Luna. Now, Luna wasn't your average girl-next-door; she was a dreamer with a vision as vast and **infinite** as the cosmos. She aspired to race faster than the swiftest gust of wind, outpace a shooting star, and claim a gleaming gold medal at the most magnificent spectacle of the Olympic Games.

As dusk descended each day, the sun making way for the moon's reign over the night sky, Luna would close her eyes and let her imagination take the reins. Within the theatre of her mind, she crafted an image as vibrant and alive as a rainbow gracing the sky after a summer drizzle. This magical moment brought about joy in her heart, fluttering like a butterfly on a warm spring day.

She saw herself racing across the finish line like a comet streaking through the night sky, her trail a glittering path of stardust. The applause from the crowd sounded like a symphony of cheers, as though every star in the cosmos had converged to celebrate her victory. And then, she envisioned herself standing atop the highest cloud, a gold medal shimmering around her neck, her national anthem resonating through the air like a sweet serenade.

Luna embodied the determination and ferocity of a lioness in pursuit of her prey across the sun-kissed savannah. She frequently visited this mental masterpiece, enhancing its details and hues until it felt as tangible as the earth beneath her feet. She trained relentlessly, pushing her limits to an extent she never thought possible, all in pursuit of her dream.

With each new dawn, Luna's faith in her abilities grew stronger. The vision of triumph etched in her mind gave her wings, propelling her skyward like a bird soaring above the clouds. And guess what? On a splendid day, under the watchful gaze of a million twinkling stars, Luna's dream blossomed into reality: she clinched the gold medal!

This enchanting story unveils the magic of visualisation. It's not merely about harbouring a dream; it's about harnessing the power of your imagination to envision yourself living that dream. By revisiting this vision persistently, you can transform your wildest dreams into tangible reality. This enchantment works for any objective, be it acing your maths exam, becoming the top video gamer in your town, or making a new chum.

No matter our dreams, approaching them with patience, confidence, and a vivid mental picture is the secret to success. So, the next time you have a dream, shut your eyes and paint it on your mind's canvas. Who knows? You might just become the next Luna!

And thus, Luna, the star runner who taught us to dream big and believe in ourselves, lived happily ever after.

The End.

Tongue Twister of this Story:

'Infinite' – This means something never ends or runs out. It's like if you had a bag of sweets that never got empty, no matter how many you ate, that would be infinite. Or imagine if you could play your favourite game all day and the fun never stopped – that's what infinite is like!

On: Vulnerability

Once upon a time, an extraordinary young lad named Max lived in a bustling town not too far away from here. Max wasn't your typical action hero, sporting bulging muscles and a steely gaze. Quite the contrary, Max was a champion of the quiet ones, a master of introverts who found solace in the pages of a good book rather than the adrenaline rush of a boxing match.

One day, when the sun was shining as bright as a thousand golden coins, his teacher, an incredibly wise woman affectionately known as Miss Smartypants, decided to shake things up a bit. With a mischievous twinkle in her eyes, she made an announcement that sent ripples of excitement through the classroom. "Class," she said, her voice ringing out clear and strong, "today's mission, should you choose to accept it, is to venture out into the vast wilderness of the playground and make a brand new friend!"

Max's heart performed a series of acrobatic flips. Make a friend? In the playground, where the rules of the jungle seemed to prevail? What if nobody liked him? What if he was left standing alone?

Taking a deep breath to steady his nerves, Max bravely stepped out into the wild unknown of the playground. His eyes fell on a girl sitting all alone under a towering tree, her gaze fixed on the branches as though they held the secrets of the universe. Intrigued, Max observed her for a moment before gathering all his courage and approaching her. In a voice barely louder than the rustle of the leaves overhead, he asked, "Hey, would you like to build a sandcastle with me?"

The girl, taken aback by Max's invitation, broke into a radiant smile that could rival the sun itself. "I'd absolutely love to!" she exclaimed. Thus, they embarked on a journey of chatter that spanned the universe – from the secret identities of superheroes to their quirky families and why pizza should be crowned as the ultimate food. As they crafted their miniature kingdom in the sand, Max found himself sharing his deepest thoughts, fears, and musings about friendship.

Now, here's where our story takes an interesting twist, dear friends. Max became a real-life superhero in that magical moment when he allowed his true feelings to shine through. By being authentic and showing his true colours, he was doing something far cooler than any muscle-bound hero could ever accomplish.

The girl, who we'll name Lily for the purpose of our story, also shared her dreams and stories. Even though they had been mere **acquaintances** that morning, by the time the sun began to set, they felt like old friends reunited. They pledged to team up again for more incredible adventures and returned home with smiles as wide as a rainbow!

That's when it dawned upon Max like a brilliant flash of lightning. Showing your vulnerabilities to others isn't a sign of weakness but a display of remarkable courage! When you are genuine, you attract friends who appreciate the real you, and the relationships you forge can be more enchanting than any spell cast by a wizard!

So there you have it, my young friends, the end of our thrilling story. Always remember, courage isn't about concealing your fears but embracing them. Honesty is indeed the best policy, and most importantly, always be unapologetically you!

And with that, they lived happily ever after.

The End.

Tongue Twister of this Story:

'Acquaintances' – You know when you meet someone at school or at the park, and you know their name and say hello when you see them, but you don't hang out with them a lot like you do with your best friends? Those people are what we call 'acquaintances'. They're not quite strangers because you know them, but they're not close friends either. They're somewhere in between – like schoolmates or your parents' friends' kids who you see sometimes. So, 'acquaintances' are people we know but don't know super well.

Final Mic Drop

Hey there, future game-changers! You've nailed it. You've got the super-duper, world-changing toolkit in your backpack now. You're ready to mould your life and this big ol' world into something even more awesome. But why park your spaceship here?

Have you ever ridden a roller coaster? You know how it's always more fun the second time around when you know where all the loops and drops are? Well, consider this your VIP pass for another ride.

Let's hit rewind and start from square one. But this time, you're not just a player; you're the game master, mini mentor, and the sauce boss. Who are you bringing on this round two? Your BFF? Your little bro or sis who sometimes drives you bananas? That cool kid who can do that crazy skateboard trick? It's your call, chief! Buckle up, and let's roll – again!

Your Mini Mentor

Ava Jacobs
@minimentors.co.uk

Tongue Twister Recap

1. **'Achilles heel'** – Imagine you're really good at playing football, but there's one thing you struggle with, like kicking the ball with your left foot. That weakness is your 'Achilles heel'. The name comes from a story about a Greek hero named Achilles who was very strong and brave but had one weak spot – his heel.
2. **'Acquaintances'** – You know when you meet someone at school or at the park, and you know their name and say hello when you see them, but you don't hang out with them a lot like you do with your best friends? Those people are what we call 'acquaintances'. They're not quite strangers because you know them, but they're not close friends either. They're somewhere in between – like schoolmates or your parents' friends' kids who you see sometimes. So, 'acquaintances' are people we know but don't know super well.
3. **'Apprehensions'** – If you have apprehensions about something, you're worried or scared about what might happen. It's like when you're nervous before your first day at a new school because you're unsure how things will go. That feeling of being sceptical and nervous is called 'apprehension'.
4. **'Audacious'** – This is a big word that describes someone brave and daring, but in a cheeky or bold way. Imagine if one of your mates decided to sing a song in front of the whole school during

assembly, even though they were told not to. That would be pretty audacious! It's like having the courage to do something that might surprise or shock people because it's so unexpected.
5. **'Aura'** – An aura is like an invisible bubble surrounding each person. Think of it like the glow around a light bulb. It's a special kind of energy that can change colours based on how we feel. For example, our aura might be bright and colourful when we're happy. When we're sad or upset, it might turn darker. Not everyone can see auras, but some believe they can sense or feel them.
6. **'Benevolence'** – This is like being the kindest and nicest person you can be. It's when you do good things for others without expecting anything in return. Imagine giving your last sweet to a friend just because you want them to be happy – that's benevolence!
7. **'Bewilderment'** – Imagine walking into a room and finding everything upside down – the chairs, the tables, even your favourite toys! You'd be really confused, wouldn't you? You wouldn't know why it happened or what to do next. That feeling of being very confused and not knowing what is going on is called 'bewilderment'.
8. **'Biases'** – You know how sometimes when you're choosing between two things, like maybe chocolate and vanilla ice cream, and you really, really like chocolate more than vanilla, so you always pick chocolate? That's a bit like what 'biases' means. It's when we prefer one thing over another, not because it's better or right but

just because we like it more for some reason. Sometimes, this can be unfair, especially when dealing with people. So, trying not to let our biases decide for us is essential.

9. **'Catastrophe'** – This is a word used to describe something really bad that happens. Imagine if you built a huge tower out of your favourite building blocks, and suddenly, it all falls down. That could feel like a catastrophe. It's a big word for a big problem or disaster.

10. **'Concocting'** – Imagine you're in the kitchen with all sorts of ingredients like flour, sugar, eggs, and butter. You decide to mix them all in a bowl, maybe add some chocolate chips too, and then bake them in the oven. What comes out? A delicious cookie! That's what 'concocting' means – mixing different things to create something new and interesting, just like you did with the ingredients to make your cookie.

11. **'Conspiratorially'** – This is a word that describes when people are secretly planning something together, usually something naughty or mischievous. Imagine if you and your mates whisper together to plan a surprise birthday party for your teacher without her knowing – that's doing something conspiratorially!

12. **'Contemplation'** – This is when you take some time to think really deeply about something. Imagine you're trying to decide what present to buy for your best mate's birthday. You might sit quietly, thinking about everything they like, what they already have, and what might make them the happiest. That's contemplation!

13. **'Curmudgeon'** – This is a word we use to describe someone who is often grumpy, a bit like how you might feel when you have to do your chores before playing with your toys. This person usually likes to complain about things and doesn't smile much. Do you know how Mr Scrooge behaves in the stories? That's a good example of a curmudgeon!
14. **'Delectable'** – We use this word to describe something that's really, really yummy. It's like when you take a bite of your favourite chocolate cake, and it tastes so good that you can't help but say, "Mmm, this is delectable!" It's like saying something is so delicious you can't get enough of it.
15. **'Diligently'** – This fancy word means doing something carefully and giving it your full attention. Think about when you're playing a game and really want to win, so you focus and try your best – that's being diligent! Or when you're doing your homework, and you make sure every answer is correct before you finish, you're working diligently. It's like being a superhero of hard work and focus!
16. **'Disseminate'** – This is a word that means spreading something far and wide. Imagine making a cool drawing and wanting all your friends to see it. You'd be disseminating your drawing if you showed it to everyone in your school or even sent copies to other schools!
17. **'Effervescent'** – Imagine opening a bottle of fizzy drink like lemonade. Do you see all those tiny bubbles popping up and dancing around?

That's what 'effervescent' means. It's bubbly, lively, and energetic, just like those bubbles!

18. **'Elixir'** – This is a bit like a magical potion. Imagine if you were playing a video game and you found a special drink that could make your character stronger, healthier, or even give them special powers – that's kind of what an elixir is. In real life, people sometimes call medicines or other things that are meant to improve your health 'elixirs'. But remember, in real life, not all potions or 'elixirs' you might hear about actually work, so it's always important to listen to doctors and grown-ups about what is safe to take!

19. **'Embodying'** – This is a bit like when you act out a character from your favourite book or movie. You're not just pretending to be that character; you're trying to think, feel and behave exactly like them. It's as if you've become that character. That's what 'embodying' means – you're making something, like an idea or quality, a part of who you are.

20. **'Enigmatic'** – Imagine you've got a puzzle box that's difficult to open because it has many secret compartments and hidden latches. You're unsure how to solve it; it's a bit of a mystery. That's what 'enigmatic' means. It's used to describe something or someone that's a bit puzzling or mysterious because they're not easy to understand.

21. **'Enlightenment'** – You know when you're trying to solve a tough puzzle and suddenly understand how all the pieces fit together?

That moment of understanding is a bit like 'enlightenment'. It's a fancy word we use to describe the feeling when you learn something new that makes you see things differently and more clearly. Everything becomes easier to see and understand, like switching on a light in a dark room. That's 'enlightenment'!

22. **'Epiphany'** – This is like a light bulb moment. It's when you suddenly understand something that you didn't get before. It's like figuring out the answer to a tricky puzzle that has been confusing you for a while. Imagine you're trying to solve a tough maths problem, and then, suddenly, you get it – that's an epiphany!

23. **'Exuberant'** – This is a big word that means you're full of energy, excitement, and happiness. It's like when you feel so joyful and lively that you can't help but jump around or laugh out loud. Imagine how you feel on your birthday morning when you're super excited about the presents and the party – that's being exuberant!

24. **'Heirloom'** – This is a special item that has been in your family for a very long time, usually passed down from one generation to the next. It could be something like your great-grandma's favourite necklace or your grandad's old watch. These items are not just valuable because they might be made of expensive materials, but they're also precious because they carry lots of family memories and history with them.

25. **'Hieroglyphics'** – These are a bit like secret codes or special pictures that people in ancient Egypt used as writing a long time ago. Instead of

letters and words, as we use now, they would draw symbols or little pictures to tell stories or send messages. So, if you ever see a picture of an eye, a bird, or a strange symbol on an old Egyptian wall or piece of paper, you're looking at hieroglyphics!

26. **'Impromptu'** – This means something you haven't planned or prepared for; it just happens suddenly. It's like when you're playing in the park and suddenly decide to start a football game with your friends. You didn't plan it before you left home; it just happened – that's an impromptu football game. It's all about doing things spontaneously, without any planning ahead.

27. **'Indispensable'** – Imagine you have a favourite toy you always play with and can't think of having fun without it. 'Indispensable' is just a fancy word for something just like that –something or someone so important you can't do without. It's like your favourite toy is 'indispensable' to your playtime!

28. **'Industrious'** – You know how some people are always busy doing things, like homework or chores, and they hardly ever sit still because they're always finding something productive to do? That's what we call 'industrious'. It's like being a busy bee who's always making honey. So, if someone is 'industrious', they work hard and are really good at getting things done.

29. **'Infinite'** – This means something never ends or runs out. It's like if you had a bag of sweets that never got empty, no matter how many you ate,

that would be infinite. Or imagine if you could play your favourite game all day and the fun never stopped – that's what infinite is like!

30. **'Insatiable'** – Imagine you really love ice cream, and no matter how much you eat, you still want more. You never seem to get enough of it. That's what 'insatiable' means – when you want more and more of something and are never completely satisfied or full.

31. **'Invigorated'** – Imagine you're feeling exhausted after a long day of playing, and then you have a nice rest, eat a yummy dinner, and suddenly you feel full of energy again, ready to play some more. That's what 'invigorated' means – it's like a recharge for your body or mind, making you feel strong and full of life again!

32. **'Mantra'** – A mantra is a bit like a special sentence or phrase people repeat to themselves. Imagine feeling a bit scared before a big football match, and you repeatedly tell yourself, "I can do this; I'm brave" – that's a bit like a mantra. It's used to help people feel better, more focused, or even calm.

33. **'Metamorphosed'** – This is a big word that means something has changed a lot. Imagine if you drew a picture and then used your coloured pencils to change it completely – it would have metamorphosed! A good example is a caterpillar turning into a butterfly. That's a huge change. So, we say the caterpillar has 'metamorphosed' into a butterfly.

34. **'Meticulous'** – Imagine if you're colouring a picture and you make sure to stay inside the

lines. Or maybe when you tidy your room and put each toy back precisely where it belongs. When you take your time to do something very carefully and pay lots of attention to every little detail, that's what we call being 'meticulous'. It's like being super careful and precise!

35. **'Ominous'** – This is a word we use to describe something that makes you feel like something bad is going to happen. It's like seeing dark clouds in the sky and thinking it will storm soon. So, if something feels or looks 'ominous', it feels or looks like it might not be very nice or could cause trouble.

36. **'Permeate'** – This means to spread or soak through something completely. Imagine dropping a bit of food colouring into a glass of water. You'll see the colour spread out; eventually, it fills the whole glass. That's what 'permeate' means – just like how the colour fills the water, anything that permeates spreads or soaks through something else.

37. **'Pessimism'** – This is when someone often thinks that bad things will happen. It's like when you always expect it to rain, even on a sunny day, or think your football team will lose before the match even starts. Pessimists often see the glass as half empty, not half full.

38. **'Prestigious'** – This is a big word that means something or someone is very well-known and respected. It's like when your favourite footballer wins the 'player of the year' award; they become prestigious because many people admire them. Or if you win first place in the school spelling

bee, that's prestigious because you worked hard and did better than everyone else!
39. **'Prodigy'** – Okay, so you know how some kids are really, really good at something? Like they can play the piano beautifully even though they're still young, or they can solve super difficult maths problems that even some adults can't do? That's what we call a 'prodigy'. It's like being a superhero, but instead of flying or super strength, their special power is being amazing at something like music, maths, or sports.
40. **'Reciprocity'** – Let's say you share your toys with your friend today, and tomorrow they share their toys with you. That's called 'reciprocity'. It's like an unspoken rule of being fair and kind to each other. So, if you do something nice for someone, they'll do something nice for you in return. That's reciprocity!
41. **'Rejuvenated'** – Imagine if you have a really old, tired teddy bear, and one day, you give it a good wash, sew up any tears, and fluff up its stuffing. Suddenly, your teddy bear looks almost new again, as if it's just had a long, refreshing sleep. That's what 'rejuvenated' means – it's when something old or tired is made to look or feel fresh and lively again.
42. **'Reminisce'** – This is when you think back to fun times or special moments that have happened in the past. Imagine if you've had a really fun day at the seaside, and later, when you're back home, you start to remember how much fun you had building sandcastles, eating ice cream, and splashing in the water. That's

called reminiscing – it's like replaying happy memories in your mind, almost like watching your favourite film again!

43. **'Reverberated'** – Imagine you're in a big room or a hall, and you shout, "Hello!" You'll hear your own voice come back to you, right? That's because your voice bounces off the walls and returns to you. This bouncing back of sound is what we call 'reverberated'. So, when a sound is 'reverberated', it means it's echoing or bouncing back.

44. **'Sagacious'** – This is a big word, isn't it? Imagine you have a friend who is really good at figuring things out, like solving tough puzzles or knowing the best time to cross the road safely. They always seem to make smart decisions. That's what 'sagacious' means – being very wise or clever.

45. **'Steadfast'** – It simply means to be very determined or unchanging in your purpose. Imagine if you're trying to learn to ride a bike, and even if you fall off a few times, you keep getting back on and trying again because you really want to learn – that's being 'steadfast'. You're sticking to your goal no matter what happens.

46. **'Sugarcoating'** – This is a term we use when someone tells a story or gives information in a way that makes it seem nicer or less harsh than it really is. Just like when you coat or cover something with sugar to make it taste sweet, 'sugarcoating' is when someone tries to make something that might be unpleasant or difficult to

hear easier to accept. It's like if you had to take a bitter medicine and your mum put a bit of honey on the spoon to make it taste better. That's what we call 'sugarcoating'.
47. **'Tempests'** – This is another word for really big, wild storms. Imagine the wind blowing so hard it could almost push you over and rain pouring down like buckets of water from the sky; that's a tempest! It's like the biggest, loudest, wettest storm you could imagine!
48. **'Tempestuous'** – Imagine a really stormy day when the wind is howling, and the rain is lashing down. Everything outside seems wild and rowdy. Well, when something or someone is 'tempestuous', it means they're just like that storm – wild, energetic, and maybe a bit unpredictable!
49. **'Unyielding'** – Imagine your favourite superhero who never gives up, no matter how tough things get. They keep going and never let anything stop them. That's what 'unyielding' means – not giving up or not changing, even when things are really hard.
50. **'Valiant'** – This is a fancy word to describe a very brave and courageous person. Imagine a knight in shiny armour, standing tall and fearless, ready to protect his kingdom from a dragon. That knight is being valiant. He's not scared, even though he might face something big and scary. So, when you're being strong and brave, even when something seems to

The End

"Think of the world as a giant colouring book filled with loads of exciting journeys. It's just waiting for brave adventurers like you to fill it in with your own special crayons."

Ava A.S. Jacobs